HOT ROD
RECORD BREAKERS

HOT ROD
RECORD BREAKERS

Melvyn Record

THE DEFINITIVE GUIDE TO THE FASTEST- ACCELERATING CARS EVER MADE

CHARTWELL
BOOKS, INC.

A QUINTET BOOK

Published by Chartwell Books
A Division of Book Sales, Inc.
110 Enterprise Avenue
Secaucus, New Jersey 07094

ISBN 1-55521-775-3

This book was designed and produced by
Quintet Publishing Limited
6 Blundell Street
London N7 9BH

Creative Director: Richard Dewing
Designer: Stuart Walden
Project Editor: Damian Thompson
Editor: John Clark
Editorial Adviser: Lorraine Gunter
Picture Researchers:
Leslie Lovett and Melvyn Record

Typeset in Great Britain by
Central Southern Typesetters, Eastbourne
Manufactured in Hong Kong by
Regent Publishing Services Limited
Printed in Hong Kong by
Leefung-Asco Printers Limited

CONTENTS

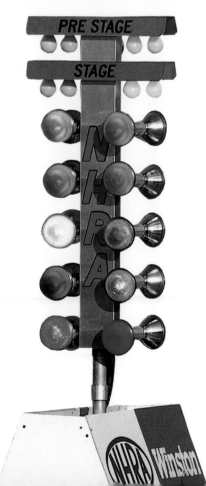

REVVING THE CHANGES

If ever a sport was destined to be full of record breakers, drag racing is that sport. Constant technological and mechanical progress has enabled these hot rods – which compete in a variety of categories, from Top Fuel to Super Street – to cover the standing-start quarter-mile in less than five seconds in 1991. In 1951, the standard run was just over 11 seconds.

Created by American hot rodders of the late 1940s and early 1950s, drag racing has progressed from an outlawed pastime to a fully-fledged motorsport boasting more than half a million competitors worldwide racing for millions of dollars in prize money.

By the mid-1960s, all but a few of the categories that are raced in today were created. During the late 1960s and most of the 1970s, the sport shed its racing-circus image and entered the 1980s as one of the more professional of all sports.

Despite competition from rival sanctioning organizations, the Los Angeles, California-based National Hot Rod Association (NHRA) and its Winston Championship Drag Racing series are the standards for all other hot-rodding and drag-racing clubs. Created by Wally Parks in 1951, the NHRA celebrated its 30th anniversary as the largest motor-sports association in the world. More than 80,000 members and a weekly drag-racing programme that allows more than 450,000 racers to compete in North America alone helps the NHRA maintain its world-leading stature.

If a first-time spectator at a drag race remembers just one image, it will be the Top Fuel dragster, the ultimate hot rod. With big wheels at the rear and small wheels at the front, the 4,000-horsepower, 295-mph (475-km/h) hot rods are indeed unchained lightning on the racetrack.

▶ **Smoke billowing from his dragster's rear tyres, Canadian Craig Smith performs all hot-rod fans' favourite pre-race ceremony: the burnout.**

ONE

SPIDER
L.R. ASSOCIATES

ATLANTA SPEED SHOP

CREW CHIEF
BOB CREITZ

GREEN LIGHT, GO!

▲ The Christmas tree, perhaps the single most symbolic image to all hot rodders. When the green light blinks, all self-respecting hot rodders mash the gas pedal.

◄ When hot rodders took their act to the dry lakes and disused airfields, their cars quickly became stripped down chassis, eventually evolving into what became known as dragsters.

Drag racing is as American as apple pie. Originally considered a temporary fad, it is one of few sports to originate in the new West to stand the test of time and be transferred to other continents.

As the sport advances towards the 21st century, racers the world over are still trying to beat the driver in the other lane to the finishing line. Far from being an exclusively American sport, racers from Australia, Britain, Finland, Norway and Sweden – to name but a few countries – have been travelling the straight-line quarter-mile since the early 1960s.

The American origins and continued American influence on the sport cannot be underestimated. Racers in Europe and Australasia aspire to be as competitive as their American counterparts. All the hardware used on their respective hot rods – from clutches to rear-wing struts and engines – originates in America. American influence is also evident in the language of the sport.

THE FIRST RACES
★ ★ ★

Reports are many and conflicting as to exactly when and where the first drag race took place. Australian Top Fuel racer Jim Read says that he read an article about "hot rods racing over a straight-line quarter-mile on Blackpool [England] pleasure beach" in a newspaper dated August 1936. No matter where the sport originated, its spiritual home is in southern California.

By the time C.J. "Pappy" Hart opened the first commercial dragstrip at Orange County Airport in Santa Ana, California, in 1951, the hot rodders already had been fine-tuning their racing techniques for 15 years or more.

▲ With their visually exciting colours and shapes – and their near unbelievable on-track performance – dragsters attract armchair hot rodders in their thousands across the world.

The first drag races were clandestine affairs, usually conducted on quiet back roads outside main towns or from one set of traffic lights to the next through town along the main drag (hence the term drag racing). Racing on the public street, however, was not popular with the local police. With their encouragement, the hot rodders were ushered to local dry lakes or to many of the abandoned airfields left in southern California after World War II.

▶ Before drag racing became the professional motor sport it is today, it was not only the race cars that were crude. Starting a dragster in the mid-1960s involved pushing it at speeds of up to 50 or 60 mph (80–95 km/h) before the engine would suddenly burst into life.

That move proved to be a blessing in disguise for the hot rodders because they were now able to express themselves more freely. Away from the confines of public roads and no longer concerned with keeping their hot rods "streetable", the cars quickly became stripped-down chassis bearing little or no resemblance to their former selves. The quest for quicker elapsed times and faster speeds became as important as beating the car in the other lane.

By the late 1940s, the sport of hot rodding – or drag racing, as it was becoming more widely known – was gaining in popularity, not just in southern California but all over the country, thanks in no small way to a new magazine created to report on this latest craze called *Hot Rod*.

WALLY PARKS – A FOUNDING FATHER

It could be argued that without Wally Parks' influence, drag racing never may have become a legitimate sport. It certainly would not have advanced to its current level of being a major motorsports activity enjoyed by hundreds of thousands of racers and fans. Parks was a test driver for General Motors before World War II, already establishing himself as a chap who liked fast cars by racing competitively at California's Muroc dry lake in the 1930s and 1940s.

Realizing that the fledgling sport of hot rodding, or drag racing, needed organizing, Parks with Ak Miller and Marvin Lee, created the National Hot Rod Association (NHRA) in 1951. They could not have known it at the time, but the NHRA would become the largest motorsports sanctioning body in the world and would continue to set the standard for straight-line performance competition as motor racing moves into the 21st century.

GOING LEGIT
★ ★ ★

One of the founding editors of *Hot Rod* magazine, Wally Parks, also had the intention of creating the National Hot Rod Association (NHRA), a club whose main task would be to bring some organization and order to the sport of drag racing.

By May 1951, the NHRA was a reality, complete with rules, membership fees, and an emblem that would become synonymous with championship drag racing. Parks' main objective was to establish the sport as a bona fide motor-racing pastime that could be conducted in as safe a fashion as possible.

From these humble beginnings was spawned the NHRA Safety Safari (originally Drag Safari), a group of NHRA founders who toured North America's dragstrips, which were springing up almost weekly, to make sure that at least the safety standards were being adhered to. In most

▲ **The NHRA Safety Safari was founded in the early 1950s to create a safe place for the hot rodders to race. Five decades later it has evolved into an organization that specializes in everything from track preparation to rescuing drivers from errant race cars.**

◄ **From a plan to get the hot rodders off the streets and into a safer environment, Wally Parks has watched the National Hot Rod Association (NHRA) grow into the largest motor racing sanctioning organization in the world.**

▶ By the mid-1970s, drag racing had long since outgrown the dry lakes and abandoned runways for purpose-built race tracks, such as Orange County International Raceway (OCIR) in California. Unfortunately for OCIR, it fell victim to ever-expanding urban development – like many other southern California racing facilities.

▼ The ultimate hot rod. Thanks to 40 years refinement, the early dragsters of the late 1940s and early 1950s have turned into 300-inch (762-cm) wheelbase, 4,000 horsepower vehicles that are the most powerful landlocked race cars on earth.

cases, the conduct of the meetings was little more than a formality, although the standards of the vehicles did leave a bit to be desired.

The quickest cars of the day were capable of covering the quarter-mile from a standing start in about 10.5 seconds with finishing-line speeds approaching 140 mph (225.30 km/h). The experts of the time calculated that the quickest a vehicle would ever cover the track would be in around nine seconds flat, with maximum speeds of around 170 mph (273.58 km/h).

During the next 35 years, drag racing grew from a sport contested by leather-jacketed hot rodders to an exhibition watched by more than a million spectators a year. Drag racing rivals Formula 1 and Championship Auto Racing Teams (CART) racing in terms of spectator appeal, and although it still cannot boast the corporate interest of those two types of competition, NHRA Championship Drag Racing manages to net more than $18-million per year series. Parks' dream of legitimizing the sport has long since been realized.

► Tom Hoover, destined to become one of drag racing's truly international stars in the early 1980s, started his career behind the wheel of a front-engined dragster in the late 1960s. The car was capable of mid-six-second performances with speeds approaching 230 mph (370 km/h).

▲ By 1972 rear-engined dragsters were the fashion and were much quicker than their front-engined predecessors. Once thought to be an impossible number to achieve, Tommy Ivo recorded the sport's first sub-six-second run, a 5.97, in October 1972.

OTHER OFFICIAL BODIES

★ ★ ★

Of course, not all drag racing is sanctioned by the NHRA. Racers dissatisfied with the NHRA way of doing things created their own organizations, including the original Professional Racers Organization (PRO), the American Hot Rod Association (AHRA) – both of which are now defunct – the American Drag Racing Association (ADRA), and the International Hot Rod Association (IHRA). Outside the United States, using the NHRA guidelines as a yardstick, the Australian National Drag Racing Association, the New Zealand Hot Rod Association, the Swedish Hot Rod Association, and dozens of British organizing clubs have been formed as a result of increasing interest.

But when it comes to big-league drag racing, there really is only one official body: the NHRA. Despite attempts by several organizations to emulate what the NHRA had achieved – most notably by the IHRA and by PRO – all their efforts counted for nought. Their inevitable failure only made the NHRA even stronger than it had been.

ONWARD AND UPWARD

★ ★ ★

Through the 1960s and 1970s, drag racing's popularity continued to grow. Racers, spurred on by the quest for quicker cars and faster times, became increasingly addicted to speed. Tommy Ivo, a television personality in the mid-1950s, recorded the sport's first sub-six-second elapsed time, prompting Cragar wheel company to create the 5-Second Club, open to the first 16 drivers who recorded a five-second elapsed time. The 5-Second Club was a sign of corporate America's growing interest in drag racing; it was also a sign that Cragar, whose wheels the hot rodders had been using for years, recognized its roots.

After that first five-second run in October 1972 it took less than two years for the Club to be complete. By June 1974, the 16 places had been filled.

Another indication that corporate America liked what it saw in drag racing came when R.J. Reynolds, through its Winston cigarette brand, became a series sponsor in 1975. Before Winston's involvement, the year's drag-racing champions had been crowned on the basis of the

CRAGAR 5-SECOND CLUB

In 1972, Cragar Industries formed the Cragar 5-Second Club, an exclusive association open to the first 16 drivers to record a sub-six second lap. Given the sport's limited progress at the time — and relatively primitive technology — the club was filled surprisingly quickly.

Almost 16 years later, Cragar would create the 4-Second Club, open to the first 16 drivers to record a sub-five-second lap — a number considered impossible back in the heady days of 1972.

1	TOMMY IVO	5.97	22 Oct. 1972
2	MIKE SNIVELY	5.97	17 Nov. 1972
3	DON MOODY	5.91	17 Nov. 1972
4	DON GARLITS	5.95	7 July 1973
5	GARY BECK	5.96	3 Sept. 1973
6	JAMES WARREN	5.97	13 Oct. 1973
7	LARRY DIXON	5.94	16 Nov. 1973
8	DAN RICHENS	5.93	16 Nov. 1973
9	JOHN STEWART	5.92	16 Nov. 1973
10	PETER KALB	5.96	26 Jan. 1973
11	JERRY RUTH	5.95	27 Jan. 1973
12	DWIGHT SALISBURY	5.97	2 Feb. 1973
13	DWIGHT HUGHES	5.97	2 Feb. 1973
14	CARL OLSON	5.94	10 March 1974
15	GARY RITTER	5.84	23 March 1974
16	FRANK BRADLEY	5.96	29 June 1974

▶ Drag racing took a major leap forward when R.J. Reynolds, through its Winston tobacco brand, entered the sport as a series sponsor. In its first year of sponsorship, Winston paid out a total of $100,000 to drag racing's end-of-year Champions. In 1990 Joe Amato received $150,000 just for winning the Top Fuel eliminator title.

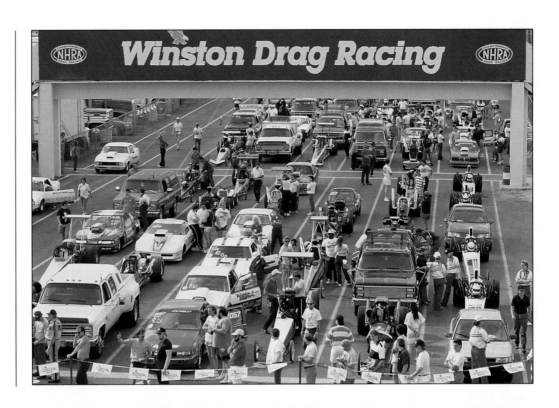

SHIRLEY MULDOWNEY – *1980 WINSTON TOP FUEL CHAMPION*

Muldowney had already caused more than a few waves when she won the 1977 Winston Top Fuel Championship. When she won the title again in 1980, Muldowney became the first two-time Top Fuel Champion in history, a feat that earned her some long overdue recognition from the media.

Muldowney had been on the racing scene for many years, earning her licence in the late-1960s before teaming with crew chief/boyfriend Connie Kalitta in the early-1970s. After a couple of semi-serious Funny Car fires, Muldowney made the change to the wire-wheeled dragsters.

Her second Championship came the hard way. Muldowney and Kalitta split up, and her husband-to-be, Rahn Tobler, took the team to NHRA National event victories at the Winternationals, Springnationals and Fallnationals on the way to the title.

CHASSIS: Ron Attebury
ENGINE: 8 cylinder aluminium Dodge
CAPACITY: 490 cu in (8.0 L)
COMPUTER-CALCULATED HORSEPOWER: 3,000 bhp @ 6,800 rpm
CYLINDER HEADS: 2-valve Stage II
FUEL CONSUMED PER RUN: 1.03 gallons per second
TYRES: Goodyear
SPONSORS: Valvoline
BEST TIME: 5.80 seconds
BEST SPEED: 247.25 mph
EVENT VICTORIES:
Winternationals 5.94 seconds 247.25 mph; Springnationals 6.04 seconds 233.16 mph; Fallnationals 5.84 seconds 241.93 mph; Winston Finals 5.95 seconds 241.28 mph

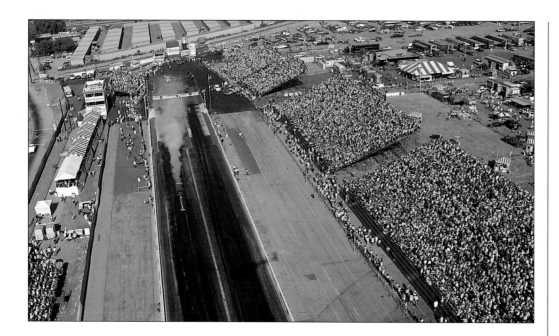

result of a season-ending drag race. For a racer who had been dominant all year, the seson could grind to a halt in the first round of eliminations because of mechanical failure.

In 1975, all that changed. A points-earning system was introduced that rewarded the year's most consistent driver. Such a system does allow a driver to win the Championship without actually winning a single event, as was the case when Rob Bruins won the 1979 Top Fuel title after finishing in runner-up position at three NHRA National events during the year.

▲ In terms of spectator appeal, drag racing ranks third behind Indy Car racing and NASCAR as the most popular motorsport in North America. At Pomona Raceway, 30 miles (48 km) east of Los Angeles, one-day crowds in excess of 50,000 are not uncommon.

STRIKING GOLD
★ ★ ★

But it was in the 1980s that drag racing, through the increased efforts of the NHRA, really hit the big time. The National event schedule was expanded from six to its current 18, and each race boasted a $1-million or more event purse (including contingency awards). Title rights were sold for each event – excluding the prestigious U.S. Nationals – as more companies recognized the potential rewards of sponsoring a major drag-racing event. And perhaps most important, the facilities were upgraded, making a day at the drag races an enjoyable and comfortable outing for the whole family, not just the hard-core fans.

At the beginning of the 1980 decade, just more than 35,000 members filled the NHRA roster. By 1991, that figure had more than doubled, approaching 80,000 by year's end and making the NHRA the largest motorsports organization in the world. To further prove the sport's increasing popularity, drag racing currently ranks third in terms of overall spectator attendance after North America's two biggest: Indy Car racing and National Association of Stock Car Racing (NASCAR).

► A total of 18 national events made up the NHRA race calendar in 1991, with the tour boasting more than $18 million in cash and contingency awards for racers to pursue. Perhaps it is partly these high stakes that make the sport so popular, as this shot of Houston Raceway Park, Texas, attests. A total of 1.5 million fans filed through the NHRA turnstiles in 1991, making drag-racing the third most popular motor sport in North America, behind NASCAR and Indy-car racing.

SITTING COMFORTABLY

★ ★ ★

Racetrack development during the 1970s can be described by one word: minimal. Performances were getting increasingly quicker and faster, and the racetracks, many of which were built in the late 1950s and early 1960s, were struggling to keep pace with the vehicles that raced on them. With the exception of Pueblo Motorsports Park in Pueblo, Colorado, and Jackson County Sports Park in Medford, Oregon, no "from the ground-up" facilities of note were constructed.

By the beginning of the 1980s, the NHRA realized that if drag racing was ever to become a major-league sport, facilities had to be improved. Dallas Gardner, NHRA president, talked of the need for drag racing's "ballparks" to improve the standards of the 1960s and enter the high-tech era of the 1980s and 1990s.

The NHRA decided to lead by example and purchased Indianapolis Raceway Park in Clermont, Indiana (approximately 5 miles – 3 km – from the famed Indy 500 course) and Gainesville Raceway in Gaines-ville, Florida early in the decade and immediately set about upgrading each facility. The racetrack owners responded to Gardner's call, and many updated their tracks to handle cars capable of accelerating from zero to 290 mph (466.70 km/h) in less than five seconds.

In 1985, a year before the opening of the Texas Motorplex in Ennis, Texas, the NHRA had commissioned a survey targeted at National event spectators, the results of which were very revealing. The activities on the track and in the pits received grades of A, but the facilities

themselves were given marks as low as C- or D. Even more alarming for the NHRA, most tracks reported that more than 30 per cent of their ticket buyers were first-time attenders but their races were growing by only 4 or 5 per cent. People liked what they saw but they were just not coming back, seemingly because of the facilities. The Texas Motorplex – and the accompanying supertrack era that its construction began – changed that trend.

The first of the supertracks opened its gates in 1986. Former Funny Car racer Billy Meyer financed the construction of the Texas Motorplex, a purpose-built facility that has stadium-style seating and an all-concrete racetrack, which ultimately yielded the first Top Fuel run within the four-second bracket.

Other supertracks followed, including Memphis International Motor-sports Park in Memphis, Tennessee; Houston Raceway Park in Houston, Texas; and Heartland Park Topeka in Topeka, Kansas, a $25-million project that includes a road course but features the dragstrip and all its accompanying amenities as the highlight of the facility. Existing tracks were upgraded, including Atlanta Dragway in Commerce, Georgia, and Bandimere Speedway in Denver, Colorado, to previously undreamed-of standards.

But the road to the future was not without disappointments along the way, the most glaring of which was the inability to build a new track in southern California, leaving the sport's spiritual home without a first-class drag racing facility because all the previous tracks had been swallowed by urban sprawl.

◄ **The Texas Motorplex.** Built by former Funny Car racer Billy Meyer, it was the first of drag racing's super tracks, complete with stadium-style seating and talking scoreboards. The track also featured a unique all-concrete race surface which ultimately yielded the sport's first four-second run.

▶ Apart from their continued support for drag racer Kenny Bernstein, Budweiser also sponsor three race-within-a-race programmes, of which the Big Bud Funny Car Shootout is one.

THIS BUD'S FOR YOU
★ ★ ★

Anheuser-Busch, through its Budweiser beer brand, has been involved with the NHRA since 1975, when it sponsored the NHRA's first Diamond P Sports (a production company created by NHRA Vice-Chairman Harvey Palash to produce motor sports shows) syndicated television show. Today, Budweiser is one of the sport's larger backers, not only sponsoring Kenny Bernstein's Top Fuel dragster, but also backing three race-within-a-race programmes: the Budweiser Classic for Top Fuel drivers, the Budweiser Big Bud Shootout for Funny Car racers, and the Budweiser Challenge for Pro Stock drivers.

The Budweiser programme was born out of a relationship between a group of wholesalers and Bernstein. Budweiser's belief in drag racing as a viable market for its product helped that relationship grow to the current situation, where Budweiser ranks second in prominence only to series sponsor Winston.

Bernstein is the key to Budweiser's continued involvement and high profile in the sport. His car is prominently featured in pre-race advertising, and Bernstein makes numerous television and radio appearances promoting his sponsor and the event. The fact that he and the car are a winning combination also helps.

LIGHTS, CAMERA, ACTION
★ ★ ★

The impact of television coverage on the overall growth of drag racing in North America cannot be underestimated. When a racer approaches a potential sponsor, one of the first questions he or she is invariably asked is: "How much television exposure does the sport receive?"

◀ and ▲ Budweiser's involvement in drag racing is substantial, enough to make the Anheuser-Busch brewery the sport's second-largest sponsor after Winston.

▶ Winston and Budweiser are not the only sponsors in drag racing. Numerous after-market parts manufacturers and the big three car makers in Detroit recognize the enormous size of the hot-rodding market and have a presence at most NHRA National events.

◀ Television's impact on the sport has been tremendous, especially since the mid-1980s. The presence of television, mainly through the Diamond P production company, has helped to attract previously reluctant sponsors to the sport, while expert analysis from big-name personalities such as Don Garlits keeps the viewers entertained.

Today, the answer is simple: a lot. But that has not always been the case. The NHRA and Diamond P limped through the early 1980s, content with their usual four syndicated telecasts, a bit of network exposure here and there, and some cable shows.

But with the growth of cable television in the United States and as the motorsports arena became a popular source of programming, the need to televise all of the NHRA National events became evident. The NHRA had a great product, a great production company, and enough money to reach that goal by the mid-1980s. Negotiations for airing of certain events with the all-sports cable channel ESPN were concluded successfully and now, in addition to all 18 National events reaching television screens across North America, the NHRA has its own weekly television programme, *NHRA Today*, which is broadcast on The Nashville Network (TNN).

Television's influence does not end in North America. With cable and satellite television now a reality across Europe, drag racing is seen around the globe. European races can be seen by viewers in the United States, allowing for an exhilarating exchange of drag-racing television programming.

LIGHTING UP
★ ★ ★

When Winston became series sponsor in 1975, drag racing was changed for ever. The racers were now racing for a pot of gold at the end of the rainbow. Admittedly, it was not much of a pot in the early days; Winston's total end-of-season payout in 1975 was $100,000, with $10,000 going to the Top Fuel Champion (Don Garlits).

But over the course of the following 15 years, the pot of gold continued to increase. By 1980, it had grown to $236,000. By 1986, it was $449,000. In March 1988, at the Gatornationals at Gainesville Raceway in Gainesville, Florida, Winston announced its $1-million sponsorship of NHRA Championship Drag Racing, with $150,000 being awarded to the 1988 Top Fuel Champion (Joe Amato).

Winston's motorsports involvement is not restricted just to drag racing. It is also the primary sponsor of NASCAR, in which America's best stock-car racers battle it out during the season for the Winston Cup – a name synonymous with the sport. Without Winston's involvement in drag racing, it is unlikely that the straight-line sport would enjoy the high profile it does today.

TWO

"BIG DADDY"
★ ★ ★

If one man's name is synonymous with drag racing, it is that of Don "Big Daddy" Garlits. A drag racer since the mid-1950s, Garlits' influence on the sport is still felt today even though he no longer races. Winner of 35 NHRA National event titles during a career spanning nearly 30 years, Garlits has spread the word of drag racing across the globe and inspired racers in Europe and Australia.

Garlits is credited with making the rear-engined dragster as popular as it is today after he changed to one following a clutch explosion in his slingshot dragster at Lions Dragstrip in California in 1971. Although the rear-engine concept had been tried several times before, Garlits was the first racer to make the configuration successful.

By the 1980s, Top Fuel dragsters had stagnated and the class was slowly but surely dying a death of chronic lack of interest. Don Garlits

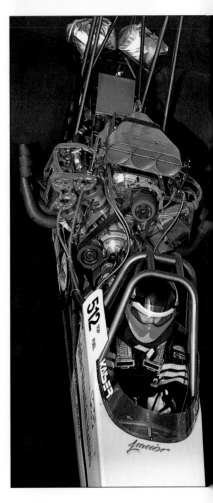

▲ Primitive by 1990s standards, Don Garlits' Wynn's Charger dragster was the standard bearer when the sport entered the 1980s. With this car Garlits set one of the longest-standing performance records in drag-racing history, a 5.63-second lap at the 1975 Winston Finals. The run was the fastest ever recorded for more than six years.

▶ Compared to Don Garlits' 1975 record-breaking dragster, Junior Kaiser's Top Fuel entry looks as though it comes from another century. About the only thing the two cars have in common is that they are of similar configuration.

◀ No one person had his name on more race cars than Keith Black; his aluminium Chrysler V-8-based engined powered more dragsters than any other manufacturer's. A former boat racer, Black turned his attentions to the ever-expanding hot rod market in the early 1950s and remained the sport's leading engine supplier through four decades. Black died on May 13, 1991.

had established a National elapsed time record for the class at 5.637 seconds four-and-a-half years earlier on 11 October 1975 at the Ontario Motor Speedway, California, and drivers had yet to better it.

"The reason that my 5.63 held up for so long was that I was doing some things (mechanically) that were not normal," Garlits explained. Garlits was running a lot of compression, a larger volume of fuel, more overdrive on the supercharger, and more ignition. He also had a higher

◀ Apart from Keith Black, the sport's other engine builder of note was the late Joe Pisano. Creator of the JP-1 aluminium Chrysler-based engine, Pisano also specialized in piston manufacture. Pisano died in late July, 1991.

gear ratio and was running a special set of tyres that he had recently obtained in Indianapolis.

"Unfortunately, I wasn't able to continue with that combination because it was extremely hard on parts. I ruined two motors at that (Ontario) event. We didn't have the connecting rods or fuel pumps to withstand what I was trying to do, and I was running a set of stock Dodge aluminum heads."

NHRA 250-MPH CLUB

For reasons that seemed like a good idea at the time, the NHRA created the 250-mph Club, which would honour the first eight drivers to exceed that magic speed (equal to 402.33 km/h). It took a long time for the Club to be filled — longer perhaps than even the NHRA anticipated. Don Garlits recorded the historic first speed of more than 250 mph, 250.69 (403.44 km/h) at the 1975 World Finals, and it took until Mark Oswald ran 256.41 (412.64 km/h) in the Candies & Hughes dragster at the 1982 NorthStar Nationals for the Club to be filled.

Perhaps the most impressive member of the Club is Billy Meyer, whose 254.95-mph (410.29-km/h) clocking at the 1982 Summernationals was recorded in his Funny Car, the only car of its class to make the Club.

Also of interest, Jerry Ruth's 255.68-mph (411.47-km/h) lap was recorded in one of Garlits' dragsters while "Big Daddy" was racing at a match race in England.

		mph	km/h	
1	DON GARLITS	250.69	403.44	11 Oct. 1975
2	JERRY RUTH	255.68	411.47	9 July 1977
3	RICHARD THARP	250.69	403.44	3 Sept. 1977
4	S. MULDOWNEY	255.58	411.30	3 Feb. 1978
5	GARY BECK	250.00	402.33	7 Oct. 1978
6	DAVE UYEHARA	250.00	402.33	7 Oct. 1978
7	BILLY MEYER	254.95	410.29	17 July 1982
8	MARK OSWALD	256.41	412.64	20 Aug. 1982

▶ By the turn of the 1980s, Shirley Muldowney had replaced Don Garlits as the sport's resident superstar. Garlits had retired, and Ms Muldowney quickly dominated the sport. However, her 1980 Winston Championship winning car was not as quick as Garlits' 1975 entry.

Another factor hurting Garlits was the lack of a major sponsor, so he had to stop his expensive experiments with parts before the car bled him completely dry.

After his victory at the 1975 World Finals, Garlits all but disappeared off the face of the earth. Dissatisfied with the way NHRA was running the sport, he retired (as he did many times), then returned and ran primarily in the AHRA ranks, although he did make occasional appearances at NHRA National events in the early 1980s.

MAN AHEAD OF HIS TIME
★ ★ ★

By the dawn of the new decade, Garlits was experimenting with a big-nosed entry, dubbed Godzilla by the motorsports press. But he was still no closer to bettering his own 5.63-second record. The closest he came was at the 1982 Gatornationals, one of those occasional visits to the NHRA tour, when he recorded 5.72 seconds.

Shirley Muldowney had replaced Garlits as the sport's resident superstar. The charismatic racer from Michigan had already won the 1977 Winston Top Fuel title, and won it again in 1980.

As testimony to today's advanced technology, Muldowney's Championship-winning car would have trouble qualifying for an Alcohol Dragster field in the 1990s. Her 1980 Valvoline-backed dragster boasted a 250-inch (635-cm) wheelbase chassis from Ron Attebury's workshop. It had a stubby rear wing, a two-speed transmission, and a

◀ In 1991, Joe Amato's Valvoline dragster was five feet (152 cm) longer than Garlits' 1975 Wynn's Charger, and would have been even longer if NHRA rules did not restrict the cars to a 300-inch (762-cm) maximum wheelbase. Amato's car was also considerably faster, having recorded a 4.87-second lap during early-season testing at Bakersfield Raceway in California.

JEB ALLEN – *1981 WINSTON TOP FUEL CHAMPION*

When Jeb Allen won the 1972 Summernationals, he was just 17 years old and on his way to a successful career as a Top Fuel dragster racer. Nine years later, when he drove his Praying Mantis dragster to the Winston Top Fuel title, Allen had become recognized as a force to be reckoned with.

Allen was hot right from the beginning, winning the season-opening Winternationals by beating Marvin Graham in the final. At the Gatornationals, Allen hit 5.62 seconds, 250.69 mph (403.44 km/h) during qualifying to become the first driver to eclipse Don Garlits' six-year record run of 5.63. Further notable victories followed at the Cajun Nationals, Mile-High Nationals and Golden Gate Nationals.

Allen's bank account began to dry up towards the end of the season, and he was forced to take a conservative approach to his racing operation. That enabled Shirley Muldowney and, towards the end of the season, Gary Beck, to close the gap at the head of the points table.

However, when Muldowney lost in the first round of eliminations at the season-ending Winston Finals and Beck failed to set Top Speed of the Meet in the final round against Dwight Salisbury, Allen was crowned Champion by just 31 points – an exciting finale to a three-horse contest.

CHASSIS: Ron Attebury
ENGINE: 8 cylinder aluminium Keith Black
CAPACITY: 484 cu in (7.9 L)
COMPUTER-CALCULATED HORSEPOWER: 3,000 bhp @ 6,800 rpm
CYLINDER HEADS: 2-valve Stage II
FUEL CONSUMED PER RUN: 1.06 gallons per second
TYRES: Goodyear
SPONSORS: English Leather
BEST TIME: 5.62 seconds
BEST SPEED: 254.23 mph
EVENT VICTORIES:
Winternationals 5.92 seconds 229.59 mph; Mile-High Nationals 5.94 seconds 243.24 mph; Golden Gate Nationals 14.46 seconds 49.80 mph

◄ **Many attempts have been made at refining, and even improving on the current drag racing power plant that evolved from an aluminium Chrysler V-8. The Australian McGee Brothers' engine is a quad-cam unit that burns an enormous amount of fuel, but is also somewhat heavy on parts. The experimental engine ran a 5.08-second best at the 1989 Winternationals.**

◄ **(Inset) The aluminium V-8 engine requires a substantial amount of attention, particularly between rounds of racing, when everything is inspected on the engine to check for any burns or scuffs. This kind of maintenance has been one of the reasons for the increased performance and consistency of the top-fuel dragsters.**

is from a Mini Metro. Basically, the only things the two have in common are four wheels, a steering wheel and a driver's seat.

Amato's Valvoline-backed dragster has a 300-inch (762-cm) wheel-base (the maximum allowed by NHRA rules), a swept-back rear wing that has been designed for aerodynamic efficiency, a direct-drive transmission, and a multi-stage clutch that feeds in groups of fingers in stages to maximize its effectiveness. The nitromethane is forced into the engine by two fuel pumps, each of which is capable of pumping more than 25 gallons (94.63 litres) per minute. The air/fuel mixture is ignited by two magnetos (with two spark plugs per cylinder). This set-up is capable of taking Amato from one end of the track to the other in less than five seconds at almost 300 mph (482.79 km/h).

Garlits was essentially five years ahead of his time, and because no racer seemed capable of approaching Garlits' performance, fans and racers lost interest in the class.

However, all hope was not lost on the Kings of the Sport, as the Top Fuel dragsters have become known. Chassis builder Al Swindahl,

flimsy clutch. The nitromethane fuel was fed into the engine by a single fuel pump, and the air/fuel mixture was ignited by a single magneto. On a good run, Muldowney would stop the clocks at somewhere around 5.80 seconds with finishing-line speeds of approximately 250 mph (402.33 km/h).

The car that carried Joe Amato to the 1990 Winston title is as far removed from Muldowney's Championship-winning entry as a Ferrari

whose cars would eventually dominate in the 1980s, saw the first of his cars win an NHRA National event when Jerry Ruth won the 1980 Mile-High Nationals in one of the unusual cars; they were unusual because of the driver's seating position which was more upright than lying down. After Canadian Terry Capp won the 1980 U.S. Nationals in another Swindahl-built car, orders began rolling in to the Tacoma, Washington, chassis maker, led by Top Fuel's best-financed operation, the Candies & Hughes team and its driver, Richard Tharp.

Garlits' 5.63 stood the test of time until March 1981, when Jeb Allen, on his way to the Winston Top Fuel title, hit a 5.62 at the Gatornationals. By the year's end, racers had recorded 10 sub-5.70-second runs, all of which were capped by Canadian Gary Beck, who recorded a 5.573 at the season-ending Winston Finals in October.

PUMP UP THE VOLUME
★ ★ ★

It did not take the nitro racers long to learn that in drag racing if some is good and more is better, then too much must be just enough. That was especially true when it came to fuel volume. The more fuel that could be crammed into a cylinder and burn, the greater the power output.

Sid Waterman, a racer turned fuel-pump manufacturer, had cornered this particular area of the market. His Big Red pump was the key to Gary Beck's 5.39-second lap in 1983, and Billy Meyer's success in a Funny Car. Beck and Meyer were his two original high-volume fuel-pump customers.

Soon the racers figured that if one pump was good, then two, logically, must be better. By 1985, Big Red had outlived its usefulness and racers such as Kenny Bernstein, Tom McEwen, and Connie Kalitta were experimenting with two pumps, although they were using the lower volume Enderle units. It was not until that year's U.S. Nationals, however, that the true potential of dual pumps was realized. Former Funny Car Champion Raymond Beadle utilized the Enderle dual-metering system on his Blue Max entry that helped driver John Lombardo push aside the opposition. Bernstein won the Budweiser Big Bud Shootout competition, and McEwen was the low qualifier in Funny Car with a 5.67, an elapsed time that three years earlier had been difficult for even a Top Fuel dragster to achieve.

Top fuel racers, understandably, jumped onto the twin-pump bandwagon, and the new system was credited with helping Beck end a 15-month winless stretch at the 1985 Winston Finals.

Tim Richards, crew chief on the Joe Amato entry and destined to become the fuel tuner of the early 1990s, tried the twin pumps along with feeding the fuel lines directly into the cylinder heads.

But tuning the fuel-delivery system was still very much a hit-and-miss affair – as it remains today – and racers like Don Garlits, Gene Snow and Dick LaHaie stuck with the single pump and were still competitive. However, by the turn of the decade, dual pumps and in-head cylinder injection were mandatory for a racer to compete with the cream of the competition. A complex series of check valves and return lines have replaced the once simple set-ups.

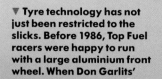

▼ Tyre technology has not just been restricted to the slicks. Before 1986, Top Fuel racers were happy to run with a large aluminium front wheel. When Don Garlits' popularized the little front wheel, Goodyear went back to the drawing board and built a tyre capable of withstanding 300 mph (483 km/h) finishing-line speeds.

SHIRLEY MULDOWNEY – *1982 WINSTON TOP FUEL CHAMPION*

Before 1980, when Shirley Muldowney did it, no one had won the Winston Top Fuel title twice. But by the end of 1982, she had already done it three times. With an Al Swindahl-built race car and sponsorship from domestic electronics giant Pioneer, Muldowney was all but unstoppable in her record-setting third Championship season.

The year did not get off to the best of starts – Muldowney stalled the engine after the burn-out in the final round of the season-opening Winternationals. But from then on, the car was unbeatable, scoring victories at the Gatornationals,

Springnationals, NorthStar Nationals and the U.S. Nationals.

The 1982 season, however, was to be Muldowney's last major one. A monumental crash at the 1984 Le Grandnational in Canada left her with badly broken legs and massive internal injuries. As a testament to her mental strength, as well as her physical fortitude, she refused to give in to the injuries. In 1986, she made a well-publicized return to the sport. On-track success was difficult to find, and Muldowney did not return to the winner's circle until late 1989, at the NHRA Fallnationals.

CHASSIS: Al Swindahl
ENGINE: 8 cylinder aluminium Dodge
CAPACITY: 490 cu in (8.0 L)
COMPUTER-CALCULATED HORSEPOWER: 3,500 bhp @ 6,800 rpm
CYLINDER HEADS: 2-valve Stage II
FUEL CONSUMED PER RUN: 1.07 gallons per second
TYRES: Goodyear
SPONSORS: Pioneer/Valvoline
BEST TIME: 5.56 seconds
BEST SPEED: 252.80 mph
EVENT VICTORIES:
Gatornationals 5.866 seconds 240.00 mph; Springnationals 5.771 seconds 233.16 mph; NorthStar Nationals 5.676 seconds 251.39 mph; U.S. Nationals 5.570 seconds 251.39 mph

KENNY BERNSTEIN – THE KING'S SUCCESSOR

In a sense, Kenny Bernstein, with no small amount of help from his talented crew chief, Dale Armstrong, has replaced Don Garlits as the king of drag racing.

Bernstein's ascension to the throne did not occur, however, until the latter half of the 1980s. Before winning his first Winston Funny Car Championship in 1985, Bernstein was better known as the racer who brought big-time corporate sponsorship into the sport. As the decade wore on, the native Texan increasingly became known as a tough competitor; he was a racer who matured from being a loser to some of the Funny Car category's big stars in the early 1980s to one who could not be beaten by the time the decade closed.

In winning four consecutive Winston Funny Car Championships (1985 to 1988), Bernstein took his career National event win record to 30. Then, in September 1989, he did the unthinkable. He announced he was going Top Fuel racing.

Bernstein's first season in the 300-inch (762-cm) wheelbase category was not a happy one. Bernstein and crew struggled through the entire season, reaching the final round only once, at the 1990 Mile-High Nationals, where they were runner-up to Joe Amato – not an easy adjustment for a team used to winning. However, changing to a Swindahl-built car at the beginning of the 1991 season reversed Bernstein's fortunes, and by September he had scored five National event Top Fuel victories.

▲ Back in the early 1970s, the fuel was ignited by a spark from a single magneto. There was not nearly the same volume of fuel to be burned as there is in a 1990s engine.

LIGHT MY FIRE
★ ★ ★

Pumping extra fuel into the engine is one thing, but burning it all is another. Extra fuel is no use unless it can all be burned, so racers began turning up the wick in the ignition department.

By 1983 the father-and-son team of Connie and Scott Kalitta was already experimenting with 16-plug heads (two spark plugs for each cylinder). When dual fuel-pump fever hit in 1985, so did the nearly obligatory use of dual magnetos to ignite the fuel.

In 1986, Bernstein and his crew chief, former Funny Car racer Dale Armstrong, introduced a set of heads that could accommodate three spark plugs per cylinder. Another Funny Car racer, Billy Meyer, even tried a four-plug head.

Realizing that things were going to get out of hand without a set standard, the NHRA introduced a two-plugs-per-cylinder rule. By 1987, even hard-core single magneto users such as Garlits were using the dual-magneto set-up.

▶ If two magnetos are better, then three must be just enough — or so racers thought. This triple-magneto set (with three spark plugs per cylinder) appeared on Kenny Bernstein's Funny Car early 1986. The unit was quickly legislated out by the NHRA, who feared the racers would get carried away and not stop until they had one magneto per cylinder.

▼ With the introduction of twin fuel pumps, racers found they could not burn the extra fuel fast enough. That particular problem accelerated the introduction of the twin magneto.

◀ Using aerodynamic trickery, a huge rear wing for stability and a 500-cubic inch engine that guzzles nitro-methane, today's modern Top Fuel dragster is the equivalent of a landlocked missile. Pictured, Jim Head.

GARY BECK – 1983 WINSTON TOP FUEL CHAMPION

There is little argument that 1983 was the year of Gary Beck. Driving Larry Minor's number one car, Beck overcame the opposition like no one had done before and no one has done since. On the way to taking the 1983 Championship title, Beck won four National events: The Gatornationals, Southern Nationals, U.S. Nationals and Golden Gate Nationals. He

also set Low Elapsed Time at 10 of the 12 National events held during the season, and he recorded the 17 quickest times in Top Fuel history to that point.

Amazingly, as dominant as Beck was in 1983, he was never to be a factor in the Championship race throughout the rest of his career, and left the Minor team before the 1986 season was over.

CHASSIS: Al Swindahl
ENGINE: 8 cylinder aluminium Keith Black
CAPACITY: 484 cu in (7.9 L)
COMPUTER-CALCULATED HORSEPOWER: 3,500 bhp @ 6,800 rpm
CYLINDER HEADS: 2-valve Dart
FUEL CONSUMED PER RUN: 1.11 gallons per second
TYRES: Goodyear
SPONSORS: Larry Minor Racing
BEST TIME: 5.391 seconds
BEST SPEED: 252.10 mph
EVENT VICTORIES:
Gatornationals 5.49 seconds 251.39 mph; Southern Nationals 5.53 seconds 249.30 mph; Golden Gate Nationals 5.39 seconds 252.10 mph; U.S. Nationals 5.50 seconds 248.61 mph

I'LL HUFF AND I'LL PUFF
★ ★ ★

In the mid-1980s, Norm Drazy, a mechanical engineer, adapted an industrial screw compressor to run as a drag-racing supercharger. The PSI, as it was called (named after Drazy's company, Performance Systems Inc.), was instantly more efficient than previous types. Employing male and female rotors, the PSI compressed air internally before discharging into the manifold.

After the PSI made its debut on Mark Niver's Alcohol Dragster in July 1988, Gary Southern surprised everyone at that year's U.S. Nationals by running a 6.12-second best in his Alcohol Dragster with the PSI. After that race, every big-name alcohol racer ordered a PSI unit.

But the PSI's success was short-lived. Niver's car exploded a unit in July 1989, sending parts hundreds of feet into the air. Despite the mandated use of blower-restraint straps and ballistic bags, another PSI exploded on Mike Troxel's Alcohol Dragster in October 1989, and the PSI was history.

▲ **Perhaps the ultimate in supercharger development was Norm Drazy's PSI screw-type unit. Far more efficient than the conventional Roots-type blower, the PSI dramatically improved the** **performance of all cars it ran on. Its success was short-lived, however, as a succession of unexplained explosions led to the PSI being banned.**

COMMANDER DATA
★ ★ ★

In the early days of hot rodding and drag racing, the crew chief relied on the driver to tell him what had happened on a particular run. He would then make the necessary tuning changes based on that information. But as elapsed times plummeted and speeds soared, things were happening too quickly for the driver to remember everything.

Data recorders provided the relief the teams were looking for. Several hit the sport in the early 1980s, designed to take the guesswork out of tuning a high-horsepower race car.

Don Prudhomme introduced a CEHCO recorder on his Funny Car at the 1982 Grand Premier event at Orange County International Raceway in Los Angeles, California. A primitive unit, it logged exhaust temperatures and took fuel-pressure readings, basically recording if and when the engine dropped a cylinder or was running too rich or too lean.

Top Fuel racer Ron Smith had the next improvement in data recorders. His self-designed unit measured engine and driveshaft rpm (which provided clutch-slippage data), fuel- and supercharger-pressure readings, and throttle-pedal pressure. The car was also fitted with a fifth wheel to measure ground speed and rear-tyre growth.

Yet it was another unit that was destined to become the standard bearer during the decade, and again it was on Bernstein's Funny Car. Co-designed by Armstrong and Jim Faust, a prototype of the now immensely popular RacePak unit was on Bernstein's car as early as 1982.

The first unit was not terribly successful, but after consulting with Unlimited Hydroplane boat racer Ron Armstrong, co-owner of Race-Pak, things quickly changed. A new, refined version of the RacePak was in Bernstein's car for the beginning of the 1984 season, and it revolutionized drag-racing data recording. The RacePak monitored and stored 32 functions, including engine rpm, rear-axle speed, tyre spin, clutch slippage, supercharger pressure, manifold pressure and cylinder pressure.

By 1985, the RacePak was available to every racer for about $2,500, and the resultant data changed the face of drag racing. It led to more efficient clutch and fuel systems, spawned high-gear-only total-clutch-management drivetrains, and aerodynamic fine tuning.

▼ When on-board data recorders were introduced to the sport in the mid-1980s, the complexion of drag racing was forever changed.

Gone was the guesswork of the past. Crew chiefs and drivers were able to get an instant replay of their last lap — errors and all.

Throughout most of the 1960s and 1970s the supercharger remained much the same as it had been when it first appeared at the drag strip — that is, a primitive 6.71:1 unit more commonly used on trucks.

BLOW IT!
★ ★ ★

The 1980s began with the 10.71:1 supercharger as the blower of choice. Although crude – its original use was on trucks – it had been refined throughout the years and was still the best way of moving vast amounts of air into the engine without any throttle lag (such as is experienced with turbocharging). With the "more is better" theory running rampant through all the other areas of fuel racing, it was only natural that the same logic would be applied to superchargers.

Meyer surprised everyone at the 1981 Orange County International Raceway Manufacturers Meet when he showed up with a 12.71:1 supercharger on his Funny Car. Today's 14.71:1 units were originally planned for use in alcohol racing, but the fuel racers saw the benefits of using the bigger superchargers and quickly adopted them. Again, fearing that things would get out of hand, as they inevitably would have, the NHRA put a 14.71:1 limit on supercharger sizes in 1983.

The 14.71:1 Roots-type supercharger, however, does have its drawbacks. The Roots pressurizes the plenum by backflow, resulting in large amounts of heat in the air while at the same time draining horsepower from the crankshaft.

The supercharger is little more than a pressure cooker, and when bolted on top of a nitro-burning engine is prone to failure, usually in the form of a fiery explosion towards the finish line.

Knowing that supercharger explosions generally begin in the intake manifold, the NHRA introduced a rule for the beginning of the 1988 season that required a burst panel on all nitro-intake manifolds. Deve-

▲ **Another item Dale Armstrong tried on Kenny Bernstein's Funny Car – never before seen – was a supercharger overdrive unit,** effectively giving the supercharger another gear. The NHRA banned the unit before it even ran on the car.

loped by fuel-systems expert Waterman, the 10-square-inch (64.5-sq-cm) panel has a limit of 195 psi (about 1.3×10^6 pascals). When pressure within the manifold reaches that level, signalling an explosion, the panel ruptures, thereby allowing the rapidly expanding gases to escape before structure separation results.

◄ **By the early 1980s supercharger technology had progressed to a stage where specialist companies were manufacturing hundreds of superchargers per day to supply the drag-racing market, including Mooneyham, Kuhl and Littlefield. The supercharger had also grown, current size/ratio being 14.71:1 as laid down by NHRA rules.**

CLUTCH PLAYER

It could be argued that the one area that has yielded the biggest single improvement in performance is the clutch. Again, it was Bernstein's crew chief, Armstrong, who identified the clutch as an area in which drag-racing performance could be improved. After two years of logging data with his RacePak computer unit on board Bernstein's Funny Car, Armstrong knew that the answer to some of his problems was the lock-up clutch. Before the arrival of the lock-up, clutches were slipping all the way down the track, wasting horsepower. What he needed was a clutch that would slip at the beginning of a run and lock up — stop slipping — as the car travelled down the track, thus more effectively transferring power from the engine to the drive train.

▶ The wear and tear on the clutch of any fuel car is tremendous, and so the maintenance of the clutch is vital to the continued performance of the car. Here one of Don Prudhomme's crewmen checks clutch plates for wear and tear.

▶ ▶ Since the NHRA introduced a "no electronics" rule during the 1990s, the multi-stages of the clutch are activated by a complicated pneumatic system.

▼ ▶ The alcohol category racers are forbidden to use a multi-stage clutch and so have to contend with varying amounts of clutch slippage. This racer uses a multitude of gauges (uncommon on most dragsters) to help him decide when to change gear.

◀ In the heat of drag racing competition, the clutch, as well as the engine, is dismantled and rebuilt in approximately 45 minutes.

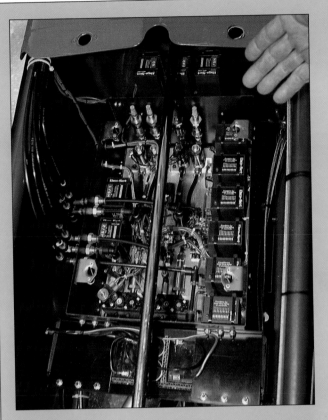

Working with Lanny and Tony Miglizzi at L&T Clutches in California in 1986, Armstrong devised a system that allowed the car to leave the starting line on the clutch's normal six fingers. Then using a button mounted on the steering wheel and connected to an air cylinder, the driver could engage three additional fingers downtrack to help the clutch to lock up.

The extra clutch stage also allowed for more precise fuel-system tuning, giving the cars with two-speed transmissions three-speed capabilities. Armstrong perfected the two-stage clutch in late 1986, which allowed Bernstein to run the first 270-mph (434.51-km/h) lap in a Funny Car.

Again applying drag-racing logic, if two stages are good, then three must be better. Although it took two years before one was used, the first three-stage clutch appeared on Meyer's Funny Car at the 1987 Winston Finals, a nine-finger unit that was activated in three stages of three.

Another clutch manufacturer, Bob Brooks of Applied Friction Techniques (AFT), had a lock-up clutch available for use as early as mid-1986. However, he was politely informed that it was too risky to run. But after Bernstein's success, ideas changed and respected crew chiefs were putting in their orders.

During the 1987 season, the trend toward high-gear-only drivelines began to emerge. Top Fuel racer Bill Mullins was the only one seriously trying the combination, but after recording a 5.39-second lap at the 1987 U.S. Nationals, AFT introduced its 12-finger clutch for use with high-gear-only set-ups. Austin Coil, crew chief on John Force's Castrol GTX Funny Car, modified an AFT three-stage into a four-stage unit for use with and without a transmission. One of the advantages of direct drive was a 40-pound (18.14-kg) weight saving from omitting the transmission. Although a lot of

racers talked about going to a high-gear-only set-up, Mullins was the only one who actually did.

Another factor in the eventual use of high-gear-only drivelines was the progressive reduction in transmission and rear-end ratios.

By the beginning of the 1988 season, fuel racers were using 15-and 10-per cent transmissions. Gear ratios that were in the 3.40:1 range in 1985 had fallen to 3.10:1 and 3.00:1 by the end of the season, and to 2.90:1 by 1989.

Gene Snow first used an AFT direct-drive high-gear-only set-up in his Top Fuel dragster at the 1988 Cajun Nationals, qualified No. 5, and within weeks was running quicker and faster than he ever had. By mid-year, most of the big names had switched to multi-shape, high-gear-only combinations from AFT or L&T.

THREE

PUSHING THE ENVELOPE

MINOR TEAM IN THE MINOR LEAGUE
★ ★ ★

Since teaming with agribusiness magnate Larry Minor at the beginning of the decade, Gary Beck had been a Winston Top Fuel Champion waiting to happen. He had been denied the title by small margins in 1980 and in 1981. Beck had also established himself as something of a barrier breaker by being the first driver to enter the 5.80-, 5.70- and 5.60-second zones, and at the close of the 1981 season, the 5.50-second zone. No one could dispute that the blue dragster, ably tuned by crew chief Bernie Fedderly, was capable of great things and spent much of its time on the track pushing the performance envelope.

In chasing the 1982 Winston Top Fuel title, Beck reset the National E.T. Record, recording a 5.54 at the 1982 U.S. Nationals. He also became the first driver to cover the standing-start quarter-mile in less than five-and-a-half seconds when he recorded a 5.48 quarter-mile later at the same race.

Despite his outstanding performance, Beck was denied the Winston title again. Shirley Muldowney, who won the 1982 U.S. Nationals title, used that victory as a springboard to her third career Championship.

However, in 1983, Beck, Minor and Fedderly were unstoppable. Minor, an experienced off-road racer, had a second car built for himself and the two cars became the terrors of the quarter-mile, qualifying at every race they attended. They even met in the final round of the 1983 Cajun Nationals, a race Minor won "by mistake".

Beck's car reset National Records again and again, and with it he scored his first event victory since the 1981 Winston Finals when he defeated Connie Kalitta for the 1983 Gatornationals title. Beck also

▲ Through 1982 and 1983 Gary Beck was all but unbeatable. The transplanted Canadian won numerous National event titles – here he is pictured after capturing the 1983 Golden Gate Nationals title – and set performance records by the score.

▼ Larry Minor racing won its second Winston Top Fuel Championship in 1987 when Dick LaHaie fought a spirited season-long campaign with Joe Amato for the title.

▲ The Gary Beck-driven,
Larry Minor-owned dragster
was a powerhouse. From
early September 1982 to
October 1983 the car
recorded the 17 quickest
elapsed times in history.

JOE AMATO – 1984 WINSTON TOP FUEL CHAMPION

CHASSIS: Al Swindahl

ENGINE: 8 cylinder aluminium Keith Black

CAPACITY: 500 cu in (8.1 L)

COMPUTER-CALCULATED HORSEPOWER: 3,500 bhp @ 6,800 rpm

CYLINDER HEADS: 2-valve Dart

FUEL CONSUMED PER RUN: 1.27 gallons per second

TYRES: Goodyear

SPONSORS: Hurst/TRW/ Keystone Automotive

BEST TIME: 5.51 seconds

BEST SPEED: 264.70 mph

EVENT VICTORIES: Gatornationals 5.544 seconds 262.39 mph; Southern Nationals 5.600 seconds 259.36 mph; NorthStar Nationals 5.534 seconds 263.15 mph

Larry Minor, whose driver, Gary Beck, had won the 1983 Top Fuel Championship so convincingly, speculated early in 1984 that Joe Amato would be "the one" in Top Fuel. How right he was.

With the freethinking Tim Richards as his crew chief, Amato, a former Alcohol Dragster racer, had recorded the sport's first 260-mph (418.42-km/h) lap on his way to the 1984 Gatornationals title. Further victories at the Southern Nationals and NorthStar Nationals cemented Amato's growing reputation as one of the best Top Fuel racers in the country.

Despite late-season charges by Beck and Don Garlits, Amato took the first of his three Championship titles in the 1980s (1984, 1988 and 1990) by a comfortable 1,800-point margin.

won the prestigious U.S. Nationals for a third time, and in doing so became the first low qualifier to win in Indy in 22 years.

On the way to claiming the Winston title, Beck set Low Elapsed Time of the Meet at 10 of the 12 National events held. He also ended the season with the distinction of having run the sport's 17 quickest elapsed times, including another barrier breaker, a first-into-the-5.30-second zone 5.391 at the 1983 Golden Gate Nationals. (The 17th-quickest run was a 5.511.) Minor was 18th quickest with a 5.513, and Beck had the 19th to 21st places. Beck's total domination earned him the Winston title by a 2,124-point margin. Former Alcohol Dragster racer Joe Amato, who had made the move to Top Fuel in 1982, finished second in the Championship chase.

Amato, a self-made millionaire of Italian descent, had been working with former Super Stock racer and engine builder Tim Richards, someone not many people had heard of. "Tim is the kind of guy that doesn't just take someone else's ideas and use them," Amato enthused; "He comes up with his own plan."

And Richards' plans were original, to say the least. During the following few years and into the 1990s, the one crew chief watched by every Top Fuel racer is Richards.

▼ **Gary Beck arrived at Minor's team with some impressive credentials, the Canadian having won the 1974 World title (the** forerunner of the Winston title), fending off Don Garlits for the honour.

THE QUICKEST 17

Beginning at the 1982 U.S. Nationals and ending at the 1983 Winston Finals, Gary Beck recorded the 17 quickest elapsed times in Top Fuel drag racing. It was a period of domination that was unmatched in its time and has yet to be bettered despite the advances in fuel-racing technology.

5.391	'83 GOLDEN GATE NATIONALS
5.391	'83 WINSTON FINALS
5.429	'83 SOUTHERN NATIONALS
5.434	'83 WORLD FINALS
5.448	'83 GATORNATIONALS
5.463	'83 NORTHSTAR NATIONALS
5.470	'83 SPRINGNATIONALS
5.471	'83 GOLDEN GATE NATIONALS
5.475	'83 NORTHSTAR NATIONALS
5.477	'83 GOLDEN GATE NATIONALS
5.484	'82 U.S. NATIONALS (1982)
5.492	'83 GATORNATIONALS
5.497	'83 GATORNATIONALS
5.500	'83 U.S. NATIONALS
5.500	'83 U.S. NATIONALS
5.503	'83 U.S. NATIONALS
5.511	'83 GOLDEN GATE NATIONALS

DON GARLITS – *1985 WINSTON TOP FUEL CHAMPION*

No one could say that they did not see it coming.

After a spectacular return to the NHRA fold at the 1984 U.S. Nationals following infrequent visits throughout the early 1980s, Don Garlits began the 1985 season as the favourite to take a second career Winston Top Fuel Championship (he also won in 1975). He did not disappoint his legions of fans.

The season got off to a shaky start when Garlits rolled his car at a match race in Phoenix, Arizona, two weeks before the season opener at Pomona Raceway in California. However, it did not take Garlits long to get into his stride. He won the first of six National event titles that year at the Southern Nationals, recording the then fastest speed in history, 265.48 mph (427.24 km/h) on his way to his title.

Further victories followed at the Cajun Nationals, Le Grandnational (where he moved into the points lead), Summernationals, U.S. Nationals and Keystone Nationals.

With a comfortable grip on the title race, Garlits, with partner Art Malone, began trying to break the 270-mph (434.51-km/h) barrier. At the season-ending Winston Finals he recorded a stunning 268.01-mph (431.31-km/h) lap during qualifying, setting the stage for a charge at the speed records when the 1986 season opened.

CHASSIS: Garlits
ENGINE: 8 cylinder aluminium JP-1
CAPACITY: 500 cu in (8.1 L)
COMPUTER-CALCULATED HORSEPOWER: 3,500 bhp @ 6,800 rpm
CYLINDER HEADS: 2-valve Dart
FUEL CONSUMED PER RUN: 1.47 gallons per second
TYRES: Goodyear
SPONSORS: Super Shops/In-N-Out Burger
BEST TIME: 5.43 seconds
BEST SPEED: 268.01 mph
EVENT VICTORIES: Southern Nationals 5.513 seconds 258.32 mph; Le Grand-national 5.489 seconds 262.39 mph; Summernationals 5.460 seconds 263.31 mph; U.S. Nationals 5.571 seconds 260.56 mph; Keystone Nationals 5.441 seconds 261.17 mph

THE CANUCK
★ ★ ★

Canadian Beck burst onto the scene in 1972 and stopped the drag-racing world dead when he won that year's U.S. Nationals title. He repeated the feat one year later, and in 1974 locked horns with Don Garlits in one of the fiercest rivalries seen in the sport, culminating in Beck's victory at the season-ending World Finals. (The season-long points-earning Winston Championship was not introduced until 1975, and World Champions were decided on the result of a single eliminator at the end of the year.)

Beck joined Minor's racing team in 1980 and immediately established himself as the man to beat in Top Fuel despite not winning the Winston Championship until 1983. Minor and Beck went their separate ways towards the end of the 1986 season, and Beck has never launched a successful comeback.

After a stint driving the McGee Brothers quad-cam Top Fueler – with comparatively little success – Beck took over as crew chief on Craig Smith's dragster and proved that he still knew how to get a car down-track by partnering his fellow Canadian to a runner-up finishing score at the 1991 Arizona Nationals.

▲ **This is the car that gave Larry Minor his first Winston title, and Gary Beck the second of his career. It also recorded the quickest run ever at that time, a 5.39 at Fremont Raceway, California.**

LARRY THE BIG RACER

★ ★ ★

Since 1980, Minor has emerged as drag racing's most prolific car owner. Not only did he own the Top Fuel dragster driven by Beck, he owns the Funny Car driven by his longtime friend Ed McCulloch.

Minor, an experienced desert off-road-racing veteran, had a dragster built for himself in 1983 and won that year's Cajun Nationals, defeating none other than Beck in the final. Beck returned the compliment a year later.

However, fielding a two-car team can lead to complications, and a first-round victory over Beck at the 1984 U.S. Nationals almost certainly cost Beck that year's Winston Top Fuel title. Of course it helped Minor's standing in the season-long points chase, in which he came sixth.

After Minor parted company with Beck, his next driver, Dick LaHaie, drove his way to the 1987 Winston title, surviving a neck-and-neck battle with Joe Amato to take the Championship at the last race of the

▲ The ever-smiling Larry Minor. Besides being one of drag racing's most prolific car owners, Minor has taken a ride or two himself and actually won a couple of National events, the 1983 Cajun Nationals (beating Gary Beck, no less), and the 1986 Mile-High Nationals.

season. When LaHaie's three-year contract with the team was not renewed, Minor signed Muldowney as the team's Top Fuel representative in 1990. But Muldowney was never a factor in the Championship battle, and after one year she, too, was dropped from the team.

Perhaps Minor's biggest disappointment has come with his Funny Car team. Headed by veteran crew chief Fedderly, the McCulloch-driven entry is a threat wherever it races and has carried the team into the winner's circle at 12 NHRA National events. But as a result of parts breakage – usually of only minor components – the car has frequently been denied the Winston Funny Car title. In 1990, the team missed the title by just 456 points.

CRUZ MISSILE

★ ★ ★

Minor's latest Top Fuel jockey is Cruz Pedregon, a young driver of undoubted talent who is following in the footsteps of his father, the late "Flaming Frank" Pedregon.

Pedregon began drag racing trucks when he was 16 years old and, with help of the late Joe Pisano, had his first ride in an Alcohol Dragster by the time he was in his early 20s. But it was not until he teamed with car owner Gary Turner in 1989 that Pedregon really came to the fore. That year, he drove the Alcohol Dragster to two National event victories.

Feeling the need to broaden his horizons, Pedregon next drove the Miner Brothers Alcohol Funny Car. Again, he proved himself a natural driver, winning in his debut in the car at the 1990 Winternationals.

After one year in the Alcohol Funny Car, Pedregon had the urge to go fuel racing, and Larry Minor just happened to be looking for a driver. The two got acquainted, and as the well-worn saying goes, the rest is history.

Driving the car that Muldowney had used the year before, Pedregon earned his Top Fuel licence with a 5.03-second lap, the quickest ever run by a new driver. But despite running 4.99 at Houston Raceway Park in testing, the car was never a winner and was dropped in mid-1991 to make way for a new Al Swindahl car. The car was a surefire winner from the moment it was unloaded, and carried Pedregon to the semifinals at the 1991 Northwest Nationals.

▼ **Larry Minor's latest driver is Cruz Pedregon. Pedregon perhaps offers Minor the most potential to repeat the heady days of the early 1980s, being one of the fastest-reacting drivers in the hot-rod world.**

▶ **For one brief year, 1990, Shirley Muldowney ran for the Larry Minor/Otter Pops Racing stable, although with little on-track success. Cruz Pedregon replaced Muldowney at the end of the 1990 season.**

▲ and ▶ The Ace in the pack. Longtime friend Ed McCulloch drives Larry Minor's Otter Pops-backed Funny Car. McCulloch, who has won numerous National event titles, has been thwarted in his attempts to win the Winston Funny Car Championship throughout his long and varied career.

PLAYING THE ACE

★ ★ ★

Known as "the Ace" McCulloch has been involved in drag racing since the early 1960s, driving everything from slingshot Top Fuel dragsters to his current Funny Car. One of the original Funny Car racers when the class was introduced in 1968, McCulloch had appeared in 38 final rounds at the close of the 1990 season, winning on 18 occasions. His first victory came at the 1971 U.S. Nationals, and his most recent was at the 1990 Winston Finals.

McCulloch teamed with Minor in 1984 after spending several seasons on the fringe of the sport driving uncompetitive cars. Since joining up with Minor, McCulloch has again become one of the most respected drivers in the class. He recorded the category's all-time quickest run of 5.132 seconds at the 1989 Chief Nationals.

If McCulloch had to pick a favourite racetrack, it would be Indianapolis Raceway Park, where he won the U.S. Nationals title five times, an event record in any category. After his initial victory in 1971, McCulloch went on to repeat the achievement in 1972, 1983, 1988 and 1990, all in the Funny Car category.

▼ The one constant on Larry Minor's team throughout the 1980s and into the 1990s has been crew chief Bernie Fedderly, left, seen here with Ed McCulloch. As crew chief on McCulloch's Funny Car, Fedderly has become one of drag racing's most respected nitro-engine tuners.

FOUR

AERODYNAMICS

◄ This experiment was a winner right from the word go. Using a huge swept-back rear wing, which created a downward force on the car, Joe Amato cracked the magic 260 mph (418.42 km/h) barrier in March 1984.

▼ Never afraid to try something different, Joe Amato raced this unusual-looking Pontiac Alcohol Funny Car during the early years of the eighties. His willingness to experiment has made him one of the sport's leading exponents.

Joe Amato was not joking when he commented that his crew chief, Tim Richards, liked to come with his own ideas. One of Richards' ideas was to consider the use of aerodynamics in drag racing – or more to the point, the current lack of use of aerodynamics.

CHEATING THE WIND
★ ★ ★

At the 1984 Gatornationals, Richards introduced an aerodynamic trick on Amato's dragster that could not be hidden. It stood out like a Mini Metro in a fleet of Ferrari F40s. It was the wing – the rear wing, to be precise. Even if they had not gone to win the 1984 Winston Top Fuel Championship, Amato and Richards would be remembered for changing the face of Top Fuel drag racing.

◄ and ▼ The rear wing on Amato's Keystone/Hurst Shifter dragster boasted a huge 7½-feet (2.29-m) tall stabilizer wing mounted high above and behind the engine.

The rear wing on Amato's Keystone/Hurst Shifter dragster boasted a huge 7½-feet (2.29-m) tall stabilizer wing mounted high above and behind the engine. The thinking behind it was so simple that the only surprise was that it had never been tried before. Situated where it was, the wing was out of the way of the turbulence created by the motor and the rear tyres, and it would act by putting downward pressure on the rear tyres. At the time, cars like Gary Beck's would burn around 400 horsepower to achieve this effect. For Amato, the wing created a situation in which the motor wasted only 100 horsepower to get the required down pressure. The saved power translated into immediate speed gains.

At that race Amato became the first person in drag-racing history to crack the 260-mph (418.42-km/h) barrier using a piston-driven engine. He ran a 5.58 at 260.11 mph (418.60 km/h) to beat Gary Ormsby in the semifinals, then ran a 5.54 at 262.39 mph (422.26 km/h) to beat Beck in the final round.

At the next race on the tour, the Southern Nationals in April, every Top Fuel racer in the pits had a crude replica of Amato's Eldon Rasmussen-designed wing. But it mattered little. Amato and Richards had caught the other racers off guard, and it was not until early spring that the field began to catch up with them.

The use of aerodynamics had been tried before. From drag racing's formative years, racers had been trying to cheat the air. None, however, had stood the world on its collective head, like Richards and Amato, and most were abandoned after a couple of appearances.

▶ and ▼ **The wing, dreamed up by crew chief Tim Richards, acted by putting downward pressure on the rear tyres — a task that hitherto wasted 400 hp of engine power.**

◀ Racers looking for an edge to cheat the wind in the early 1970s came up with front-wheel covers, known as pants. They looked good but offered little in terms of aerodynamic improvement.

TEMPO'S TIME HAD COME
★ ★ ★

Aerodynamic improvements were not restricted to the Top Fuel category. Once again, Kenny Bernstein and his crew chief, Dale Armstrong, were looking for more efficient ways to get their Ford Tempo-bodied Funny Car to cut through the air. Because of Bernstein's close ties with Ford, he became one of the first drag racers allowed to use the once inaccessible car-manufacturer's wind tunnels. After spending two days locked in the Lockheed wind tunnel, the car that emerged was one of the most advanced quarter-mile vehicles ever seen – regardless of category – and was head and shoulders more efficient than anything that had gone down a dragstrip.

The Tempo had rounded fenderwells, a lipped nose spoiler and side skirt, a belly pan, and full side windows to prevent air from getting inside and under the body. A tall rear spoiler – or whale deck as it became known – provided increased down-force without substantial drag. Bernstein's previous car, a Mercury LN-7, created 1,360 pounds (616.90 kg) of drag at 200 mph (321.86 km/h) but the Tempo created just 940 pounds (426.38 kg) at the same speed. That was an improvement of 45 per cent; the body alone was a full 10 per cent more efficient than the stock Tempo Funny Car body.

Needless to say, Bernstein, armed with this knowledge, became unbeatable in 1984, registering a third-place finish in the Winston Funny Car Championship chase before winning the first of four consecutive titles the following year.

BUICK DEBUT
★ ★ ★

Bernstein and Armstrong were not finished with aerodynamics, however. In 1987, they introduced a Buick LeSabre that looked nothing like a Funny Car (or an '87 LeSabre for that matter) ever did. It had a huge rear spoiler, a narrow roof, and a laid-back windscreen. It resembled a Porsche 962 more than a Buick. The car was legal, much to the NHRA's disappointment; it represented a rather liberal interpretation of the rules by adhering to the letter of the rulebook if not the spirit.

Perhaps the ultimate in aerodynamic efficiency, the car helped Bernstein rack up a 43-3 win-loss record from October 1986 to September 1987. In that time, he won 10 out of 12 events, and it was unquestionably Bernstein's most productive period.

Other racers duplicated Bernstein's ghastly LeSabre body, including Jim Head, John Force and Ed McCulloch. But none achieved the same success that Bernstein enjoyed. Obviously, Bernstein did not win all those races on aerodynamic trickery alone; plenty of horsepower helped to push the car through the air.

To ensure that Funny Car bodies would at least bear some resemblance to the showroom models they were based on, the NHRA clarified the 1988 body rules, and the Batmobile era was over.

At the same time as the aerodynamic trickery in the Funny Car ranks, the Top Fuel racers began looking again at what tricks would be attached to their cars to help them cheat the wind, thus spawning perhaps the sport's most creative period – the rebirth of the streamliners.

◄ (and inset) When it made its first appearance in 1987 it quickly became known as the Batmobile. Kenny Bernstein's Buick LeSabre Funny Car was the ultimate in aerodynamic efficiency – and was something of a liberal interpretation of the NHRA rule book. The car was banned in 1988.

► When Kenny Bernstein's "Batmobile" first appeared, it did not take the other Funny Car racers too long to come out with their own versions. John Force's Castrol GTX Funny Car was perhaps the least wild of the interpretations.

FUELLING THE RECOVERY

★ ★ ★

Ironically, this creative period came at a time when Top Fuel racing was at its lowest ebb. The class had been decimated in 1984.

Throughout that year the numbers of entries were down and at three races, the Springnationals, Summernationals and NorthStar Nationals, the fields fell short of the usual 16 cars. The Springnationals was further marred by a top-end spill involving racer Doug Kerhulas, who was seriously injured. Two weeks later, Shirley Muldowney had a near-fatal crash at Le Grandnational when her car jumped the guardrail just past the finishing line.

Adding to the category's woes, Amato and then number-three man in the standings, Jody Smart, ordered Funny Cars, seemingly ready to join the Candies & Hughes team, which had made the change in 1983. Number-five finisher Richard Tharp went sprint car racing. The IHRA dropped the class altogether in time for the beginning of the 1984 season, stating that there was not any interest in the category.

The category's spectacular recovery from its deathbed can be attri-

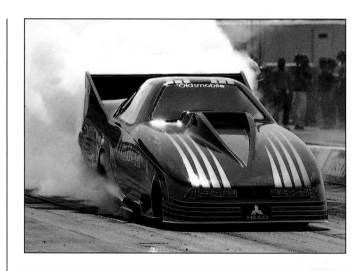

COEFFICIENT OF DRAG (Cd)

The lower the Cd number, the better an object cuts through the air — or at least, that is the theory. The lowest Cd numbers come from shapes that have the maximum body volume forward, tapering back towards the narrowest angle at the rear — in other words, a teardrop.

PARACHUTE	1.35 Cd
FLAT PLATE	1.17
CUBE	1.05
SEATED PERSON	0.60
MOTORCYCLE	0.57–0.80
CONVERTIBLE CAR	0.50–0.70
RAILWAY CARRIAGE	0.50
CITY BUS	0.45–0.50
SPORTS CAR	0.32–0.36
BIRD	0.30
BULLET	0.25–0.3
LAND SPEED RECORD CAR	0.11
TEAR DROP (3:1 length-to-thickness ratio)	0.04–0.05

▲ **Jim Head's outrageous Oldsmobile Firenza was the wildest of all the Funny Car creations, although neither his, or John Force's, could match the out-and-out performance of Kenny Bernstein's machine.**

◄ **Although many Top Fuel racers copied Joe Amato's tall rear wing, when the Key Auto Parts team introduced their car at the 1984 Gatornationals they had effectively given themselves a six-week advantage over the competition.**

buted to two incidents, unrelated except that they both occurred at the 1984 U.S. Nationals.

After sporadic visits to the NHRA tour since his "retirement" from drag racing in 1975, Don Garlits was back, with a vengeance. His last appearance had been at the 1984 Gatornationals, and he had not been heard of since. But with the help of Bradenton, Florida, track owner Art Malone, the two veterans of the sport had gathered what spares they had left and announced that they would race in Indy and at the remaining races on the tour. Better yet, they were already building a new race car for the 1985 season. As in all fairy tales a happy ending was in the script. Garlits won on his return, defeating his long-time rival, Connie Kalitta, in the final round.

The other incident was the announcement by Joe Hrudka, founder and president of Mr. Gasket, that two of his other companies, Cragar and Weld, would sponsor an exclusive Top Fuel Classic series in 1985.

Garlits and Malone remained true to their word. Besides racing at all the events in 1985, they had a sponsor, Super Shops, and pushed aside the opposition. Ever the crowd favourite, the king of the dragsters won six NHRA National events in 1985 and was crowned Winston Top Fuel Champion exactly 10 years after his first title. He then repeated the achievement in 1986, joining Muldowney as the only other three-time Winston Top Fuel Champion, and he won the U.S. Nationals title that year for an unprecedented third straight time. From his comeback in September 1984 to the end of the 1986 season, Garlits won 13 of 29 National events he entered. Top Fuel and Don Garlits were again very much alive and well.

DON GARLITS – *1986 WINSTON TOP FUEL CHAMPION*

CHASSIS: Garlits
ENGINE: 8 cylinder aluminium JP-1
CAPACITY: 500 cu in (8.1 L)
COMPUTER-CALCULATED HORSEPOWER: 3,800 bhp @ 6,800 rpm
CYLINDER HEADS: 2-valve Dart
FUEL CONSUMED PER RUN: 1.49 gallons per second
TYRES: Goodyear
SPONSORS: Super Shops/ Garlits & Malone
BEST TIME: 5.34 seconds
BEST SPEED: 272.56 mph
EVENT VICTORIES:
Gatornationals 5.503 seconds 268.65 mph; NorthStar Nationals 5.562 seconds 259.36 mph; U.S. Nationals 5.399 seconds 266.66 mph; Chief Nationals 5.390 seconds 268.01 mph

By winning the 1986 Winston Top Fuel title, beating Darrell Gwynn by 524 points, Don Garlits became only the second driver – Shirley

Muldowney being the other – to win drag racing's most prestigious Championship three times.

Garlits had already set the tone for 1986 at the close of 1985 by announcing his intentions to take a crack at the 270-mph (434.51-km/h) barrier with a car the likes of which never had been seen before.

He was true to his word. At the 1986 Gatornationals – just 20 miles (32 km) from Garlits' home town of Ocala, Florida – he introduced Swamp Rat XXX, a semi-streamliner. Much as Garlits expected, the car cracked 270 mph with consummate ease,

running as fast as 272.56 (438.63 km/h) on the way to the event title. After a second victory of the year at the Cajun Nationals, Garlits suffered his first blowover at the Summernationals. He rebuilt the car and won back-to-back titles at the NorthStar Nationals and U.S. Nationals. His last victory of the year, at the Chief Nationals, put a grip on the Winston title.

Although he did not win the Winston Finals title, Garlits did win the Cragar/Weld Wheel Top Fuel Classic title, his final achievement before a second blowover in Spokane, Washington, put him into self-imposed retirement.

1

2

THE BLOWOVER

For all the sport's potential for disaster, accidents, especially in the Top Fuel category, are few and far between. It is a testament to the NHRA's strict safety requirements that when there is a spill, the driver more often than not walks away. If an accident does occur, the cause is usually traced back to the drive. Use of on-board data recorders often proves the point. Competitors, believing they can drive their way out of trouble, sometimes stay on the throttle a millisecond too long, and . . .

When the Top Fuellers breached the 270-mph barrier, a new phenomenon started to occur. Eventually dubbed "the blowover", drivers found that the front wheels of their race cars started to lift as they approached the finish line. For drivers travelling at more than 270 mph, this could present something of a problem.

The first to experience the blowover was Don Garlits, whose Swamp Rat XXX blew over backwards at Old Bridge Township Raceway Park, New Jersey, in 1986. Many so-called experts attributed the accident to Garlits' use of a spoon-shaped nose on the front of his dragster. However, in late 1987, when Richard Holcomb went over backwards in his more conventional-looking dragster questions were raised as to whether any car might go over. Garlits, by this time, had quit the sport. Another blowover, this time at a track in Spokane, Washington, had prompted the King of the Dragsters' early retirement.

At the start of the 1989 season Eddie Hill rode out perhaps the fastest blowover, his Super Shops/Pennzoil dragster hauling its rear wing across the finish line at 250 mph before somersaulting in mid-air. Hill's prang was attributed to the front wings vibrating loose at the mid-track point and falling into a negative angle of attack – in effect, encouraging the car to lift off the ground. Other racers have since joined the infamous 360-degree club, including Don Prudhomme, the late Gary Ormsby and Russ Collins, whose BME-backed dragster performed some mid-air ballet before slamming to earth in a tangle of twisted tubing. In all cases, the drivers climbed out from what was left of their respective race cars, shaken, sometimes bruised, but very much alive.

In 1986 drag-racing fans got their first look at a new phenomenon: the blowover. First in many things, Don Garlits rode out this blowover at the 1986 NHRA Summernationals at Old Bridge Township Raceway Park, New Jersey. Paired against Darrell Gwynn in a qualifying heat, Garlits' revolutionary Swamp Rat XXX has carried the front wheels away from the starting line before snapping skywards at mid-track (1). Past the point of no return, Garlits' car starts to pivot on its rear wing (2), before turning through 180 degrees and slamming back down to earth (3). Garlits is fortunate that the car lands the correct way up. He is able to regain control of the car and bring it to a safe halt (4). Garlits was uninjured and returned to racing two weeks later.

3

4

FIVE

CHEATING THE WIND

For a year or more, racers were content to copy and refine Joe Amato's big wing idea. It worked – well – and it was not expensive. But seeing what Kenny Bernstein and Dale Armstrong were up to set many racers thinking.

Streamliners had been tried in the past, but with little success. Racers back in the 1960s and 1970s adapted their ideas from the Bonneville Salt Flat lakesters and streamliners. Those ideas were suited to cars travelling over four or five miles (5–8 km) of racecourse, but they offered few advantages for cars travelling the straight-line quarter-mile.

The racers of the mid-1980s knew that having a slippery looking race car was not enough to achieve quicker elapsed times. The slippery shape had to be effective, and several racers began looking at the Indy car set and how ground-effects might be applied to drag racing.

▲ and ▶ Streamliners had been tried in the past – with varying degrees of success, or lack of it – but when Gary Ormsby's Castrol GTX streamliner appeared in 1986 it heralded a new chapter in drag racing history.

CASTROL GTX STREAMLINER
★ ★ ★

The first racer to sink a significant amount of money into a workable streamliner was Gary Ormsby who, with help from sponsor Castrol GTX, introduced his aerodynamically advanced race car at the 1986 Winternationals.

The body was built from carbon fibre and featured an Indy Car-style cockpit. Along with the unusual nose and wing designs, this gave the car an unmistakable March-car look. The final design was the result of dimensions fed into an aircraft design computer, which provided a three-dimensional drawing and simulated wind-tunnel testing. Eloisa Garza, part of the Jim Hall/Johnny Rutherford Indy Car team that won the 1981 Indy 500, created the body, which was mounted on an Al Swindahl chassis. Without a doubt, it was an amazing vehicle that looked as though it was doing 270 mph (434.51 km/h) standing still, which was the target for the car.

As new rides usually do, the Castrol streamliner suffered from new-car troubles. At its debut at the 1986 Winternationals, the car's supercharger exploded on the burnout. The team later learned that the magnetos were earthing out on the carbon fibre bodywork, which triggered the explosion.

Then came Garlits.

CASTROL GTX STREAMLINER TECH SHEET	
CAR	Castrol GTX Special
CHASSIS	Swindahl
ENGINE	489-cubic-inch (8-litre) Keith Black
CRANKSHAFT	Crower
SUPERCHARGER	Mooneyham
INTAKE MANIFOLD	Cragar
CYLINDER HEADS	Dart
IGNITION	Mallory
SPARK PLUGS	NGK
HEADERS	Hedman
TRANSMISSION	Lenco
CLUTCH	Crower

▶ It was not too often that a racer would go the whole hog and build a complete streamliner, as Abrams and Schacker did in 1986. However, like racers before them, they found their Alcohol Dragster a little too unpredictable and retired the car before any realistic performances were turned in.

▼ Conceived with the aid of an aircraft computer, and featuring futuristic nose and wing designs, the Castrol GTX streamliner had the feel of an old-style Indy car.

DICK LAHAIE – 1987 WINSTON TOP FUEL CHAMPION

CHASSIS: Dave Uyehara
ENGINE: 8 cylinder aluminium Keith Black
CAPACITY: 484 cu in (7.9 L)
COMPUTER-CALCULATED HORSEPOWER: 4,000 bhp @ 6,800 rpm
CYLINDER HEADS: 2-valve Dart
FUEL CONSUMED PER RUN: 1.56 gallons per second
TYRES: Goodyear
SPONSORS: Miller High Life/ Larry Minor Racing
BEST TIME: 5.118 seconds
BEST SPEED: 283.55 mph
EVENT VICTORIES: Arizona Nationals 5.269 seconds 274.55 mph; Springnationals 5.359 seconds 260.64 mph; Le Grandnational 5.296 seconds 270.27 mph; Keystone Nationals 5.143 seconds 280.72 mph

Veteran racer Dick LaHaie led the 1987 Winston points chase once all season: immediately after his semifinal defeat of Joe Amato at the season-ending Winston Finals. Amato's car chewed up the transmission 150 feet (46 m) off the starting line, and LaHaie sprinted to a 5.19-second 277.17-mph (446.05-km/h) run that was worth $100,000 to LaHaie (the prize at that time for the winner of the Winston points chase).

LaHaie had been behind Amato all year, and at one point he had trailed his rival by a symbolic 1,320 points (the number of feet in a quarter-mile). But he had narrowed the gap after a three-race win sequence in the Larry Minor/Miller-backed car, scoring victories at the Cajun Nationals, Springnationals and Le Grandnational, which moved him to within 450 points of Amato.

Still, Amato would not go away. While LaHaie encountered an inexplicable tyre-spin problem, Amato further extended his points lead with victories at the Mile-High Nationals and U.S. Nationals.

By working on the fuel system and clutch-management system, LaHaie overcame his tyre-spin problems and responded with event titles at the Keystone Nationals and Fallnationals, closing the gap on Amato to just 162 points going into the Winston Finals. The semifinal victory over Amato gave LaHaie his first — and so far only — Winston Top Fuel title by a mere 42 points, the closest winning margin in the 13-year history of the Series.

SWAMP RAT TECH SHEET	
CAR	Swamp Rat XXX
CHASSIS	Garlits
ENGINE	495-cubic-inch (8.1-litre) JP-1
CRANKSHAFT	Keith Black
SUPERCHARGER	Odyssey
INTAKE MANIFOLD	Cragar
CYLINDER HEADS	Dart
IGNITION	Mallory
SPARK PLUGS	Champion
HEADERS	Hedman
TRANSMISSION	Lenco
CLUTCH	L&T

GARLITS AND THE SWAMP RAT XXX
★ ★ ★

Garlits was a man with a mission in the early part of the 1986 season. He wanted to be the first racer to break the 270-mph (434.51-km/h) barrier, and he wanted to do it badly. He had already achieved 268.01 mph (431.31 km/h) at the 1985 Winston Finals, and he had hoped to run 270 mph at the 1986 Winternationals. But his promised new car – which he claimed would turn everyone's heads – was not quite ready.

When he introduced Swamp Rat XXX at the Gatornationals a few weeks later, no one was ready for what they saw. The most notable feature on the self-built car was the nose, which was shaped like a teaspoon and housed the 14-gallon (53-litre) fuel tank. Rather than having the usual motorcycle-type front wheels, Garlits' car had spun aluminium discs that were wrapped by rubber belts (he could not get tyres small enough). The other item that caught the eye was the fully enclosed cockpit, which Garlits claimed was an aerodynamic and safety feature rolled into one. Garlits expected the Lexan shield to become standard equipment on all dragsters within six months of development, and he was proved right.

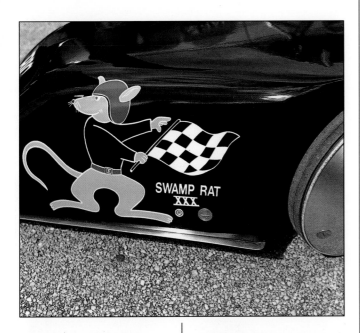

◄ **Another racer to try the canopy was Connie Kalitta. The canopy was a temporary fad, however, and by the turn of the decade few racers were using one.**

▲ ►**Not a true streamliner – it was dubbed a semi-liner by most observers – Don Garlits' Swamp Rat XXX was by far the most successful of all the attempts at cheating the wind. Distinguished by its spoon-like front nose and little front wheels, it enabled Garlits to break the 270-mph (434.51-km/h) barrier in March 1987 on the car's National event debut.**

► Streamlining 1977 style. Don Durbin raced this creation complete with the aluminium wheel tubs at that year's Winternationals; he failed to qualify. Without the tubs the hot rod ran a best of 6.02 seconds at 238 mph (383 km/h).

◄ and ▲ The "Spoon" was undoubtedly fast, but Don Garlits found out that the front wheels like to throw the rubber belts at speeds over 270 mph (434.51 km/h). Garlits cured the problem by installing a set of light-aircraft wheels on the car.

Although many people scoffed when they first saw Garlits' car, "Big Daddy" knew exactly what he was doing. His car was unquestionably a streamliner, but he had not gone the whole way and included engine canopies and rear-wheel flares. Knowing that weight would be a factor, his latest car weighed exactly the same as his previous car.

On the car's first lap, Garlits hit a 5.46 at 268.01 mph (431.31 km/h). After a one-week delay because of bad weather, Garlits beat former American football star Dan Pastorini in the semifinals, recording a 5.40 at 272.56 mph (438.63 km/h). Garlits had achieved what he had set out to do, and the streamliner's future was assured. Or so it seemed.

Garlits' car was a success, especially after he replaced the rubber belts with light aircraft wheels and tyres under the nose of the car. Despite a blowover at the Summernationals in July, Garlits came back and won five events on the way to the 1986 Winston Top Fuel title.

Ormsby's car was not so successful, and was retired after the 1987 Southern Nationals. The two cars competed twice, and both times Garlits' semi-liner, as it was becoming known, won. Their last duel was

JOE AMATO – *1988 WINSTON TOP FUEL CHAMPION*

Consistency won the 1988 Winston Top Fuel title for Joe Amato, the second of his career. Other racers were quicker than he was — most notably Eddie Hill and Gene Snow, both of whom ran in the once unthinkable four-second zone during 1988 – but Amato was a consistent late-round finisher, and that ability carried his TRW/Key Auto Parts dragster to the Championship.

Amato finished as a semifinalist or better at 13 of the 16 NHRA National events that made up the 1988 tour. He won four of them: the Summernationals, the California Nationals, the NorthStar Nationals and the U.S. Nationals (an event he had won four times by 1990). He was runner-up at three: the Winternationals, the Gatornationals and the Southern Nationals. The other drivers could simply not match his unerring consistency.

The Championship title underscored Amato's reputation as arguably the best driver in the class — especially given Garlits' self-imposed retirement — and the Pennsylvania self-made millionaire continues to be the dominant force in Top Fuel racing as the sport moves into the 21st century.

CHASSIS: Al Swindahl
ENGINE: 8 cylinder aluminium Keith Black
CAPACITY: 500 cu in (8.1 L)
COMPUTER-CALCULATED HORSEPOWER: 4,500 bhp @ 6,800 rpm
CYLINDER HEADS: 2-valve Dart
FUEL CONSUMED PER RUN: 1.59 gallons per second
TYRES: Goodyear
SPONSORS: TRW/Keystone/ Hurst
BEST TIME: 5.006 seconds
BEST SPEED: 287.35 mph
EVENT VICTORIES:
Summernationals 5.305 seconds 274.47 mph; California Nationals 5.176 seconds 274.30 mph; NorthStar Nationals 5.180 seconds 267.14 mph; U.S. Nationals 6.813 seconds 202.79 mph

◄ **On his way to the 1988 Winston Top Fuel title, Joe Amato tried several aerodynamic devices, including these sidepods mounted in front of the rear wheels. No one really knew whether they worked, but Amato liked them, anyway.**

▶ After experimenting with the spoon-shaped front nose the next thing Joe Amato tried was the canopy — as did several other racers. However, like the spoon, Amato rejected this idea and returned to running a conventional dragster.

◄ Streamlining 1991 style. At the start of the 1991 season Joe Amato experimented with this Mike Magiera-designed package which worked from the start. Without the rear wing, Amato recorded a 5.05 at Houston Raceway Park, but the package was never tried again as Amato concentrated on the Winston Championship chase.

Joe Amato was the only racer other than Garlits to try the spoon-type front nose. He ran it only once, at the 1986 NorthStar Nationals, did not like the way the car felt at the top end, and sold it to Northern California racer Butch Blair.

▶ and ▼ ▶ The Mike Magiera-designed ground-effects package was also tried on Kenny Bernstein's Top Fuel dragster during 1991. Like his rival Joe Amato, however, Bernstein tried the package on only rare occasions as he too became embroiled in a heated Winston championship title points battle.

at the 1986 Cajun Nationals, where the two met in the first – and so far only – all-streamliner final round.

Garlits' success prompted several drivers to try the streamliner route. The most notable racer to hop onto the bandwagon was Joe Amato, who introduced a car strikingly similar to Garlits', ran it once (at the 1986 NorthStar Nationals), did not like its handling characteristics at the top end, and promptly parked it forever.

Darrell Gwynn, a former Alcohol Dragster racer who had moved up to Top Fuel in 1985 and then joined forces with the Budweiser team of Kenny Bernstein, introduced a monstrous-looking streamliner at the 1987 Winternationals. The car was unbelievably heavy, and race by race more of the streamlining body panels were taken off until it looked more like a conventional dragster. Without the extra weight, the car was a flyer and chalked up unprecedented elapsed times, culminating in a 5.28 at the 1986 Chief Nationals.

The writing was on the wall. Streamliners looked good, but the extra weight added to the car could not be overcome by aerodynamic trickery. In drag racing, it was still better to bully the car down the track. Even Garlits, streamlining's strongest proponent, agreed. "It doesn't seem to be a good idea in drag racing anymore, does it?" he said.

▲ Jim Head has been running this ground-effects package on his Top Fuel dragster since the late-1980s. Similar to the Mike Magiera unit, Head has run in the 4-second range at over 280 mph (450.60 km/h) with his set-up. The covers on the wing struts are to tidy up the airflow around the struts.

▼ Wind-tunnel tests suggested Darrell Gwynn's 1987 dragster would cut through the air like a knife through butter. It probably would have, too, if it did not weigh an extra 200 pounds (90.7 kg) or more. Without the extra body panels the car was a flyer.

▶ Canadian Craig Smith had his own ideas on streamlining during 1990, running this particular package on his Alcohol Dragster during the early part of the year, with little success.

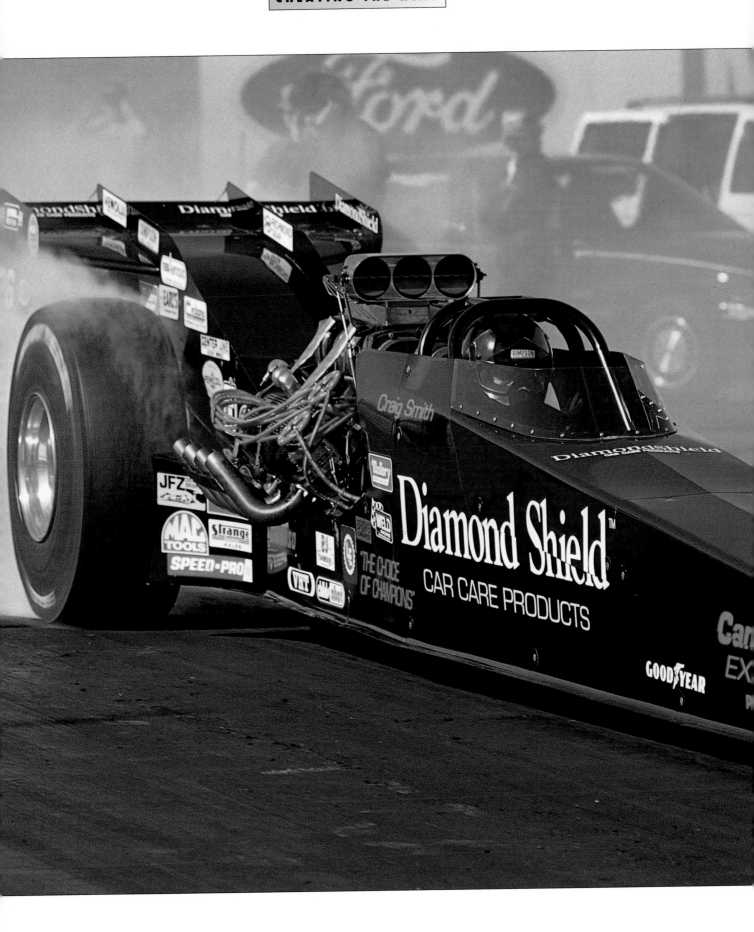

SIX

RACE TO THE FOURS

Despite the advances being made in aerodynamics, not to mention engine tuning, a sub-five-second time was still considered impossible as late as 1987.

Darrell Gwynn's 5.28 at the 1986 Chief Nationals was unquestionably amazing, but most people thought that the Top Fuel dragster had reached its peak.

THE CREW CHIEF'S SECRET
★ ★ ★

As it had been for years, the secret was in the fuel system and the clutch. If a crew chief could organize those two pieces of hardware so that one would complement the other effectively, the world was his or hers. And as he had through most of the 1980s, Dale Armstrong was leading the field once again.

Besides tuning Kenny Bernstein's Funny Car, Armstrong was providing a tune-up for Gwynn, who had joined Bernstein's Budweiser team in 1986. With Armstrong's undoubted expertise, Gwynn led the assault on the record books. At the 1987 Gatornationals, Gwynn clocked 5.22 in qualifying. A month later at the Southern Nationals, he ran even quicker, recording a 5.204-second lap. A couple of weeks later, he dipped into the teens, running a 5.176 at the Texas Motorplex during the Winston All-Stars event.

How much quicker could a Top Fuel dragster go? Dick LaHaie, who was on his way to a first – and so far only – Winston Top Fuel Championship, responded with a 5.171 at the Summernationals. Then Joe Amato, the 1984 Winston Top Fuel Champion, joined the race. Amato had already assured himself a place in the record books in early September when he recorded the sport's first 280-mph lap at the U.S. Nationals, where he reached 282.13 mph (454.03 km/h) during eliminations. With crew chief Tim Richards calling all the shots, Amato joined the race for the four-second zone at the next event on the tour, the

▲ With help from former opponent Shirley Muldowney, Don Garlits took a crack at the 4-second zone in October 1989. He fell just short, recording a career-best 5.07 on his one and only run in the car.

▼ By the end of the 1991 season, Joe Amato had run more 4-second laps than the rest of the 4-second runners combined. Much of that mechanical credit goes to his crew chief, Tim Richards, left.

Keystone Nationals. There, he recorded a 5.171 during testing, then achieved a 5.118 the next day during qualifying – the first sub-teen five-second run in history.

Anticipation was high that at the next event on the calendar, the Chief Nationals at the Texas Motorplex, a track that has become synonymous with the best elapsed times since it opened in 1986, someone would do a five-zero-second run. Amato obliged by recording a 5.090 in qualifying.

It did not stop there. That number was surpassed when, during eliminations, Gwynn again took up the challenge and achieved an even quicker 5.084.

◄ In October 1987 Joe Amato became the first driver into the 5.0-second zone when he produced an explosive 5.09 at the Texas Motorplex.

GARY ORMSBY – *1989 WINSTON TOP FUEL CHAMPION*

The late Gary Ormsby had been a fixture on the drag-racing tour since the mid-1960s, although he seldom ventured too far from his northern California home to race. That all changed in the early 1980s, when Ormsby and crew chief Lee Beard emerged as one of the sport's freethinking teams. They experimented with everything from ground-effects to full-streamliners to gain an edge over the competition.

It was not until 1989 that they discovered that edge. Beard stumbled across the perfect fuel system and clutch-management system to complement Ormsby's driving style, and the team was all but unbeatable throughout the year.

With uncanny reaction times, Ormsby drove his way to six National event titles: the Winternationals, the Super-nationals, the Mid-South Nationals, Le Grandnational, the Chief Nationals and the Winston Finals.

The Championship did not come easily. On the way to the title, Ormsby crashed two cars within four weeks: one at the California Nationals at more than 280 mph (450.60 km/h) and one at the NorthStar Nationals. After both spills, Ormsby walked away without a scratch.

The season obviously also had its high points. The highest was Ormsby's victory at the Chief Nationals, where he recorded the quickest and fastest run in the history of the sport, a 4.919 and 294.88 mph (474.55 km/h). In September 1990 Ormsby recorded a pair of even better numbers, achieving a 4.88 at 296.05 mph (476.43 km/h) at the Heartland Nationals.

After coming close to success-fully defending his title in 1990, Ormsby died of stomach cancer on 28 August 1991. He was 49 years old.

CHASSIS:	Al Swindahl
ENGINE:	8 cylinder aluminium Keith Black
CAPACITY:	489 cu in (8.0 L)
COMPUTER-CALCULATED HORSEPOWER:	4,800 bhp @ 6,800 rpm
CYLINDER HEADS:	2-valve Dart
FUEL CONSUMED PER RUN:	1.82 gallons per second
TYRES:	Goodyear
SPONSORS:	Castrol GTX
BEST TIME:	4.919 seconds
BEST SPEED:	294.88 mph

EVENT VICTORIES:
Winternationals 5.065 seconds 278.81 mph; Supernationals 5.094 seconds 278.12 mph; Mid-South Nationals 5.039 seconds 287.26 mph; Le Grandnational 5.155 seconds 278.98 mph; Chief Nationals 4.972 seconds 291.26 mph; Winston Finals 5.050 seconds 286.80 mph

▲ **The quickest and fastest run in history came at Heartland Park Topeka in Topeka, Kansas, when the late Gary Ormsby's Castrol GTX dragster hit a 4.88 at 296.05 mph (476.43 km/h).**

The late Gary Ormsby fought hard for his one and only Winston Top Fuel title in 1989. On the way he made numerous 4-second runs, including the fastest ever run at the start of the new decade, a 4.88 at 296.05 mph **(476.43 km/h) recorded at Heartland Park Topeka, Kansas, late 1990.**

AN OUTSIDER BREAKS THROUGH

★ ★ ★

When the 1988 season opened, racers were openly talking about who would run the sport's first four-second elapsed time. Many assumed it would be Amato, Gywnn or, possibly, LaHaie. Most never even considered Eddie Hill.

Hill, one of the original drag racers in the mid-1950s, had been racing drag boats for most of the 1970s and early 1980s. It was on water that he established himself as something of a speed merchant, setting track and National Records everywhere he raced. He made the fastest pass ever by a propeller-driven boat at 229.00 mph (368.53 km/h), a record that still stood in 1991.

Drag-boat racing, however, is not without its dangers. A 217-mph (349.22-km/h) spill at Firebird Lake in Arizona prompted Hill to call it a day and return to the asphalt quarter-mile. He made his return at the 1985 Mile-High Nationals. Three years later, still an outsider, Hill unleashed a 5.066 at the 1988 Gatornationals and suddenly became the favourite and the name on everyone's lips.

One month later at the Texas Motorplex, which now was run by the IHRA courtesy of Billy Meyer, Hill broke perhaps one of the last true performance barriers. On 9 April he drove his Super Shops/Pennzoil-backed dragster to a 4.990. The four-second barrier had been broken.

Hill's achievement deflated many other drivers, including Amato and Gwynn, who believed that they should have broken the four-second mark. There were no sour grapes – far from it, everyone was happy for Hill – but it certainly knocked the wind out of other racers' sails.

▲ **The four-father. Eddie Hill beat both favourites Joe Amato and Darrell Gwynn to the 4-second zone. The former drag-boat racer recorded a history-making 4.99 on 9 April 1988.**

▼ **After being the first racer into the 4-second zone, Eddie Hill amazingly "lost" his combination and struggled through 1989 and 1990 before coming back with a vengeance during the 1991 season, running fours apparently at will.**

JOE AMATO – *1990 WINSTON TOP FUEL CHAMPION*

The 1990 Winston Top Fuel title was decided in the last race of the last event of the year. In one lane was defending series Champion Gary Orsmby; Joe Amato was in

CHASSIS: Al Swindahl

ENGINE: 8 cylinder aluminium Keith Black

CAPACITY: 500 cu in (8.1 L)

COMPUTER-CALCULATED HORSEPOWER: 5,400 bhp @ 6,800 rpm

CYLINDER HEADS: 2-valve Dart

FUEL CONSUMED PER RUN: 2.02 gallons per second

TYRES: Goodyear

SPONSORS: Valvoline/Key Auto Parts

BEST TIME: 4.935 seconds

BEST SPEED: 291.26 mph

EVENT VICTORIES: Arizona Nationals 5.052 seconds 275.14 mph; Mile-High Nationals 5.102 seconds 275.48 mph; NorthStar Nationals 4.970 seconds 273.39 mph; U.S. Nationals 5.042 seconds 270.83 mph; Heartland Nationals 5.040 seconds 272.14 mph; Winston Finals 4.935 seconds 282.39 mph

the other. The racers were tied in the points chase. The winner of the quarter-mile dash would win the event and collect from Winston the $150,000 bonus cheque for the Series Champion.

The race was over before it began. Ormsby could not wait for the green light, and Amato sprinted to a 4.93 for his third Winston Top Fuel Championship. That victory put him in the lofty company of Shirley Muldowney and Don Garlits, the only other three-time winners of the Series.

Amato fought neck-and-neck with Ormsby throughout the 1990 season, in which both drivers scored six National event victories. Victories at the Arizona Nationals (formerly the Fallnationals), Mile-High Nationals, NorthStar Nationals, U.S. Nationals, Heartland Nationals and the Winston Finals were enough to earn Amato the title.

"THE SNOWMAN" STRIKES
★ ★ ★

Almost unbelievably, neither Amato nor Gwynn was the second driver into the 4-Second Club. Gene Snow, a former Funny Car racer of some renown in the early 1970s, beat them to it when he produced a 4.997 at the NHRA Supernationals at another Texas track, Houston Raceway Park. Still, it was Hill who again stole the headlines. In beating Amato in the final round of that race, Hill recorded a 4.936, a run that even as the sport moves through the 1990s remains one of the quickest of all time.

Apart from the advances made in clutch and fuel-system technology, the car's length had increased from a standard 270 inches (685.8 cm) in 1987 to 300 inches (762.00 cm) in 1988, and this helped the dragsters to break the four-second barrier. Not all racers were convinced that longer was better. Hill's car, for instance, was only 288 inches (731.52 cm) long. But for the most part, new competitive dragsters had a 300-inch chassis (the maximum allowed by the NHRA), which allowed for better engine placement.

◀ With a driving career that spans four decades, Shirley Muldowney is one of the sport's more charismatic figures, having won three Winston Top Fuel titles and numerous event titles, and has even had a movie made about her life story, "Heart Like A Wheel".

▲ With Eddie Hill's 4-second run being recorded at the Texas Motorplex – which was under IHRA management at the time – Gene Snow gave the NHRA their first 4-second run at Houston Raceway Park in October 1988.

CRAGAR 4-SECOND CLUB

Like they had 16 years earlier, when it became obvious that the Top Fuel dragsters were going to conquer yet another performance barrier, Cragar Industries formed the 4-Second Club in 1988, open to the first 16 drivers to record a sub-five second run. Eddie Hill's 4.99 was recorded at the Texas Motorplex, which was run under IHRA sanction at the time. Gene Snow had the honour of giving the NHRA its first four-second lap at Houston Raceway Park almost six months later.

▼ Shirley Muldowney became the first woman driver in the 4-second club when she achieved a 4.97 during qualifying for the 1989 Keystone Nationals at Maple Grove Raceway, Pennsylvania.

1	EDDIE HILL	4.990	9 April 1988
2	GENE SNOW	4.997	6 Oct. 1988
3	RICHARD HOLCOMB	4.998	15 Oct. 1988
4	JOE AMATO	4.996	3 March 1989
5	GARY ORMSBY	4.991	10 June 1989
6	DICK LAHAIE	4.983	3 Sept. 1989
7	DARRELL GWYNN	4.981	3 Sept. 1989
8	S. MULDOWNEY	4.974	15 Sept. 1989
9	M. BROTHERTON	4.996	7 Oct. 1989
10	FRANK BRADLEY	4.998	25 Oct. 1989
11	JIMMY NIX	4.960	16 Feb. 1990
12	LORI JOHNS	4.975	17 Feb. 1990
13	FRANK HAWLEY	4.982	4 Aug. 1990
14	T. JOHNSON Jnr.	4.964	29 Sept. 1990
15	DON PRUDHOMME	4.980	2 Feb. 1991
16	KENNY BERNSTEIN	4.996	24 Feb. 1991

JOE AMATO – *1991 WINSTON TOP FUEL CHAMPION*

CHASSIS: Al Swindahl

ENGINE: 8 cylinder aluminium Keith Black

CAPACITY: 500 cu in (8.1 L)

COMPUTER-CALCULATED HORSEPOWER: 5,400 bhp @ 6,800 rpm

CYLINDER HEADS: 2-valve Dart

FUEL CONSUMED PER RUN: 2.05 gallons per second

TYRES: Goodyear

SPONSORS: Valvoline/Key Auto Parts

BEST TIME: 4.858 seconds

BEST SPEED: 291.63 mph

EVENT VICTORIES: Gatornationals 4.897 seconds 285.98 mph; Mile-High Nationals 5.052 seconds 274.64 mph; California Nationals 4.968 seconds 277.34 mph; Northwest Nationals 4.968 seconds 279.58 mph

Who is the king of the dragsters? Joe Amato dispelled any doubts by clinching an unprecedented fourth Winston Top Fuel title in 1991. That accomplishment put him in a class by himself: before 1991, Amato, Don Garlits and Shirley Muldowney had each managed to win three crowns.

Amato's title charge began with a bang during pre-season testing at Bakersfield Raceway in California when the Tim Richards-tuned Valvoline dragster recorded a 4.87-second lap, at the time the quickest quarter-mile in the history of the sport.

Despite his car's obvious performance advantage — he set the NHRA national record at 4.897 seconds in winning the Gatornationals — Amato did not make his presence felt until the middle of the season. Back-to-back-to-back victories at the Mile-High Nationals, California Nationals and Northwest Nationals vaulted Amato into the points lead, where he stayed for the remainder of the year.

Ending the season the way he began it, Amato and crew travelled back to Bakersfield between weekends of the rain-delayed Winston Finals and achieved the quickest run ever recorded by a Top Fuel dragster at 4.858 seconds.

▼ As a drag-boat racer, Eddie Hill achieved the fastest ever recorded pass by a propeller-driven boat at 229 mph (368.53 km/h). The record still stands.

SEVEN

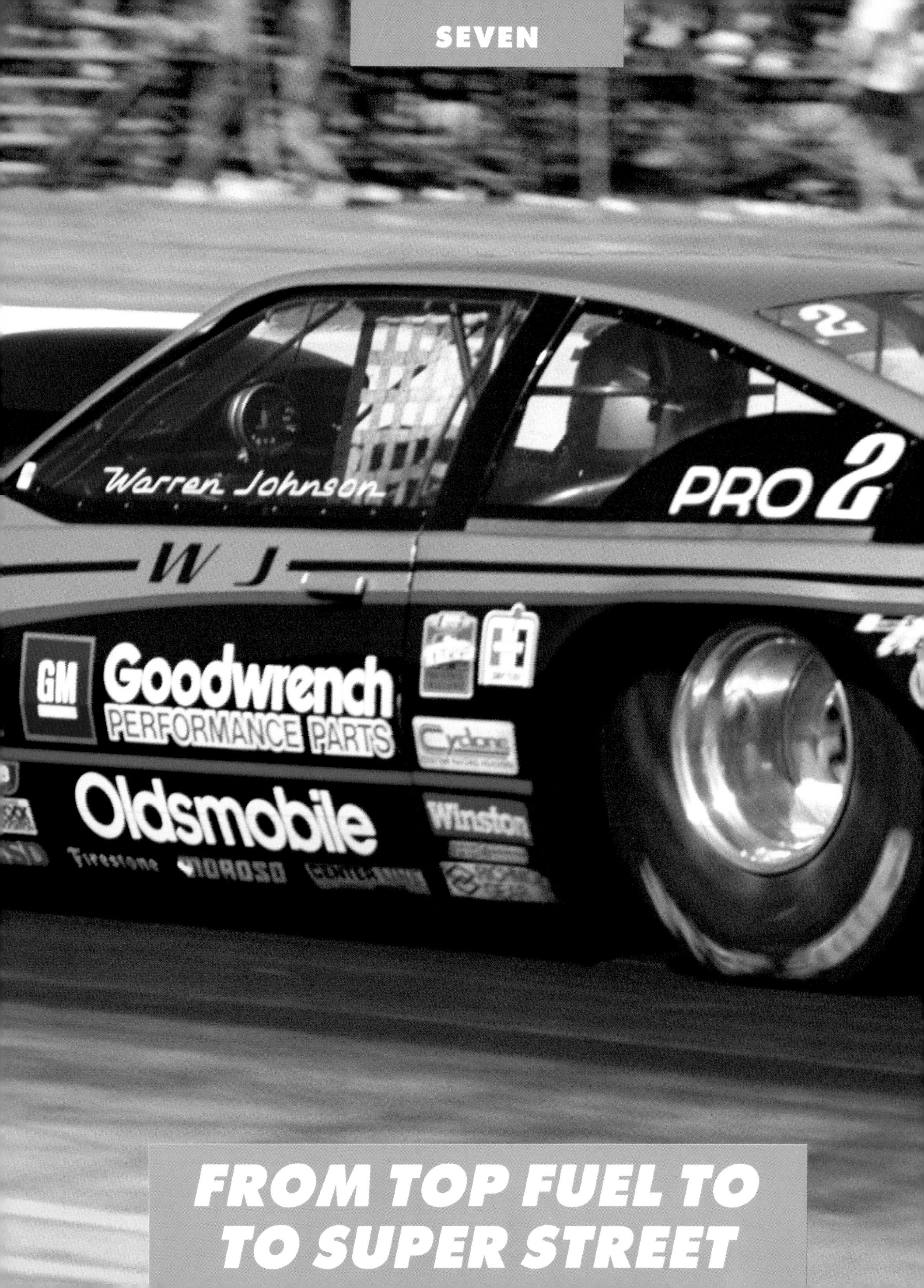

FROM TOP FUEL TO TO SUPER STREET

Although drag racing is not restricted in Top Fuel dragsters, the near-300-mph (480-km/h) landlocked missiles are indeed the sport's glamour category, much like Formula 1 cars and World of Outlaws sprint cars are the kings of the circuit races and the dirt tracks, respectively.

To cater for every driver's individual need for speed, however, the NHRA has created and nurtured 11 other categories, ranging from nitro-burning Funny Cars, capable of Top Fuel-like performance, to Pro Stock Motorcycles, the only two-wheel category recognized by the sanctioning body, to 11-second Super Street vehicles.

The categories are split into two distinct groups, Professional and Sportsman. The reasoning for the split is that the Pros – those who drive Top Fuel dragsters, Funny Cars, Pro Stockers and Pro Stock Motorcycles – race full-time for a living. The Sportsman competitors, those in Alcohol Dragster, Alcohol Funny Car, Competition Eliminator, Super Stock, Stock, Super Comp, Super Gas and Super Street, are weekend-only racers who cannot afford to make the financial commitment to racing in one of the Pro classes. This can be, however, something of a misnomer. Dozens of Sportsman racers spend a small fortune racing their cars, sometimes matching and even exceeding the amount a Professional racer would spend on his or her racing operation.

TOP FUEL

Unmistakable in appearance, the Top fuel dragster is everyone's lasting image of a dragster. It has big wheels at the rear and small wheels at the front. It is the ultimate hot rod. The 25-foot (7.62-m) vehicles are the fastest accelerating cars in the world, capable of covering the standing-start quarter-mile in 4.8 seconds at speeds in excess of 290 mph (466.70 km/h).
NHRA National Elapsed-time Record: 4.897 seconds – Joe Amato, Gainesville Raceway, Gainesville, Florida, March 1991.
NRHA National speed Record: 294.88 mph – Gary Ormsby, Texas Motorplex, Ennis, Texas, October 1989.
All National Records must be backed up within 1 per cent.

▼ **Before any race car is allowed on the track, it must first pass a rigorous technical inspection. Here, Jim White's Funny Car – the fastest of the breed with a 289.94 mph** **(466.60 km/h) lap recorded in mid-September 1991 – has his rear spoiler checked for correct height and width.**

FUNNY STORIES

★ ★ ★

When the 1980s opened, only four drivers had sat in a Funny Car and covered the quarter-mile in less than six seconds: Don Prudhomme, who ran a 5.98 at Ontario Motor Speedway in Ontario, California, in 1975; Raymond Beadle, also at 5.98 at the 1979 U.S. Nationals in Indianapolis, Indiana; Pat Foster; and Gordie Bonin. Today, more Alcohol Funny Car drivers have recorded five-second runs.

Not surprisingly, as Top Fuel performance times fell, so did those of Funny Cars. Two soon-to-be crew chiefs led the assault on the Record books at the beginning of the 1980s. Dale Armstrong (now Top Fuel driver Kenny Bernstein's crew chief) was the first into the 5.80s, and Tom Anderson (currently Funny Car driver Al Hofmann's crew chief) recorded the category's first 5.70-second lap.

Bernstein, unquestionably the Funny Car star of the 1980s, was first into the 5.60s (at 5.67), with no small amount of tuning help from Armstrong, who took over as crew chief in 1981. Rick Johnson surprised everyone when he cracked the 5.50 zone in one of Roland Leong's many entries over the years, getting a 5.58 at the 1985 Winternationals.

From there, Bernstein set the record-breaking pace. With the aid of an aerodynamically improved Ford Tempo, Bernstein managed to record the Funny Car category's first sub-5.50-second run, a 5.425 at the Texas Motorplex in 1986.

Then, with an even faster Buick LeSabre, Bernstein plunged into the 5.30s, running 5.397, 5.368 and 5.364 in the following year on 5 April, again at the Motorplex.

It was a surprise, therefore, that Bernstein was not the first Funny Car racer into the 5.20s. That honour went to Ed McCulloch, who drove the

FUNNY CAR

Although based on current Detroit models, Funny Cars bear little resemblance to their showroom counterparts. The only similarities are the tail-lights and badges. Using an identical engine to that of the Top Fuel dragster (mounted in front of the driver rather than behind), the 4,000-horsepower race cars are capable of running 5.1-second laps at speeds of just over 290 mph (466.70 km/h).
NHRA National Elapsed-time Record: 5.140 seconds – Jim White, Texas Motorplex, Ennis, Texas, October 1990.
NHRA National speed Record: 290.13 mph – Jim White, Texas Motorplex, Ennis, Texas, October 1991.
All National Records must be backed up within 1 per cent.

Larry Minor/Miller High Life Olds Cutlass to a 5.252 at Houston Raceway Park in Houston, Texas, in early October 1987. Predictably, Bernstein was not far behind. He recorded a 5.295 a couple of weeks later at Pomona Raceway in Pomona, California.

Conspicuously absent from the record books during this period of Funny Car development was one of the sport's more recognizable drivers: Don "the Snake" Prudhomme. Prudhomme had dominated the category during the mid- to late-1970s, winning an unprecedented four consecutive Funny Car titles. However, when sponsorship money began to dry up, Prudhomme became less and less competitive and sat out the 1986 season because of lack of sponsorship funds.

He returned to the sport the following year with backing from U.S. Tobacco's Skoal brand, and on 2 March 1989 recorded the category's first 5-teen, a 5.193 at Houston Raceway Park in Houston, Texas.

▶ **Long known as one of the fastest Funny Cars in the world, the JP-1 Special, campaigned by the late Joe Pisano, was unbeatable in its day. With Mike Dunn at the wheel, the car achieved the category's first recorded 280 mph (450.60 km/h) lap at the Texas Motorplex in October 1987.**

FUNNY BUT FAST

★ ★ ★

From that day in early March, elapsed times have not dropped much. The standard at the end of the 1991 season was still the 5.132 recorded by McCulloch at the 1989 Chief Nationals in Larry Minor's Miller High Life Oldsmobile Cutlass.

However, one area of Funny Car performance that constantly improved through the end of the 1991 season was finishing-line speeds. Although considerably shorter than their Top Fuel cousins, Funny Cars are far more aerodynamically efficient, able to make use of air dams, rear spoilers and other wind-cheating devices.

Bernstein was the first Funny Car racer to go more than 270 mph (434.59 km/h) with a 271.41-mph (436.78 km/h) run at the 1986 U.S. Nationals. He continued to improve the record until Mike Dunn, driving for the late Joe Pisano, arrived on the scene and quickly established himself as the speed king. Dunn, a second-generation driver who had driven a variety of Funny Cars, was the perfect complement to Pisano's undoubted tuning abilities. At the 1987 U.S. Nationals – on the way to his first and only Nationals title – Dunn recorded laps of 278.89 mph (448.82 km/h) and 274.64 mph (441.98 km/h). Four weeks later, at the Texas Motorplex, Dunn became the first driver to break the 280 mph (450.60 km/h) barrier with a 280.72 mph (451.76 km/h) run, backed up with a 279.93 mph (450.49 km/h) lap for the official record.

The breed's first 290-mph (466.70/km/h) run came in late 1991, again at the Motorplex. Jim White, driving Roland Leong's Hawaiian Punch Dodge Daytona, had given notice that he would probably be the first Funny Car racer to make a run at more than 290 mph with laps in excess of 289 mph (465.09 km/h) at the 1991 U.S. Nationals and Keystone Nationals. In less than perfect conditions, he recorded a 5.148-second lap coupled with a 290.13-mph (466.91-km/h) finishing-line speed to get his name in the record books.

▶ and ▼ Buddy Ingersoll's turbocharged V-6 Buick was originally built for Pro Stock competition. However, the Pro Stock racers, fearing the car would run away with the class if it ever ran well, had the car banned from their category. Ingersoll was forced to run the car in Comp eliminator and did run as quickly as 7.17-seconds, proving the Pro Stock racers' fears to be well-founded.

PRO (NOT SO) STOCK
★ ★ ★

Perhaps the most complex of drag racing's categories is Pro Stock, dubbed the factory hot rods by the sport's traditionalists. Pro Stock is one of the few categories in which Detroit's involvement is felt at a racing level. The big three American manufacturers – Ford, Dodge and General Motors – are involved in the category in some way.

At the beginning of the 1980s, the category was controlled by a complex series of weight limits, and racers were restricted to small-block power plants. In March 1980, the late Lee Shepherd recorded the quickest run ever for the petrol-burning race cars with an 8.37-second lap. At the end of the 1991 season, Warren Johnson held the National Record in one of his Oldsmobile Cutlasses at 7.180 seconds.

To be fair to Shepherd, Johnson was using a completely different engine combination with fewer restrictions than was Shepherd. In time for the beginning of the 1982 season, the NHRA made its rules like those of the IHRA – which at the time was running a successful Pro Stock Programme – and introduced a 500-cubic-inch (8.2-litre) two four-barrel carburettor rule that instantly trimmed the performance of the cars by more than a quarter of a second. Shepherd, who began the year by recording the category's quickest run, soon established himself as the class leader in the Reher-Morrison Chevrolet Camaro with a 7.86-second lap at the 1982 Winternationals.

From that race on, Shepherd and his arch rival Bob Glidden, driver of a series of Motorcraft Parts-backed Ford entries, dominated the category. Shepherd was the first into the 7.70s with a 7.78 at the 1982 Gatornationals. Seven months later, he broke the 7.60 barrier with a 7.69 at the Golden Gate Nationals. The 7.50s were not so easy to achieve. It took Shepherd more than two years to break into the zone, and his 7.59-second run recorded at the Citrus Nationals in West Palm Beach, Florida, in December 1984 was yet another record-breaking achievement to add to the list.

PRO STOCK

About the only things a modern-day Pro Stock car have in common with the showroom model it is based on are four wheels and a steering wheel. Hidden beneath the sleek fibreglass body panels are 500-cubic-inch (8.2-litre) race engines that breathe via two four-barrel carburettors. Radical chassis and suspension changes enable the cars to lap in the 7.1-second range at finishing-line speeds in excess of 190 mph (305.77 km/h).

NHRA National Elapsed-time Record: 7.180 seconds – Warren Johnson, Maple Grove Raceway, Pennsylvania, September 1991.

NHRA National Speed Record: 193.21 mph – Bob Glidden, Sears Points International Raceway, Sonoma, California, July 1991.

All National Records must be backed up within 1 per cent.

Three weeks before the 1985 Gatornationals, Shepherd was killed in a testing accident. Glidden, who had played second fiddle to his friendly rival for four years, established himself as the class leader. The first sub-7.5-second run was recorded at the 1985 Keystone Nationals as Glidden clocked a 7.497-second lap. Just less than a year later, at the 1986 U.S. Nationals, Glidden achieved a 7.377.

With the 7.4-second barrier broken, improvements were made in mere thousandths of a second as racers edged towards the 7.2-second zone. Unheralded Frank Sanchez stole everyone's thunder when he clocked a 7.294 at Houston Raceway Park in October 1988. Glidden lowered the record to 7.256, again at Houston Raceway Park, in March 1989. Mark Pawuk enjoyed his 15 minutes of fame (actually, it

▼ **Bob Glidden is the undisputed Pro Stock king. With 80 National event victories in his long career – most of them at the wheel of a Ford – he entered the 1990s** **as the driver with most wins ever in National event competition.**

lasted six months) when he recorded 7.220 at the 1990 Supernationals in his Oldsmobile Cutlass.

Then Darrell Alderman took over.

Alderman, driving the Mopar Parts/Wayne County Speed Shop Dodge Daytona, came to prominence at the end of the 1990 racing season with a string of dominating performances that ultimately carried him to the Winston Pro Stock title. In the first of these performances, he recorded a 7.206 at Heartland Park Topeka during the Heartland Nationals. One week later, while competing at the Texas Motorplex, he lowered the record even further, to 7.184, to astound everyone. John-

son's 7.180, at the 1991 Keystone Nationals, is the only quicker run.

Johnson, however, is the undisputed king of the finishing line, where the Georgia engine builder regularly clocks up Top Speed honours. Johnson was the first Pro Stock racer to go more than 180 mph (289.67 km/h) with a 181.08-mph (291.41-km/h) run at the 1982 Golden Gate Nationals. Glidden beat Johnson to the 190-mph (305.77-km/h) barrier with a 191.32-mph (307.89-km/h) run at the 1987 U.S. Nationals, and is still the National Record holder at 193.72 (311.75 km/h), recorded at the 1991 California Nationals. However, Johnson has recorded more runs in excess of 190 mph than most other Pro Stock racers combined.

TWO WHEELS ON MY WAGON
★ ★ ★

It is called a Professional category, but just how professional is it? Pro Stock Motorcycle suffers from a unique identity crisis. The NHRA touts the class as the two-wheel equivalent of Pro Stock, although the big four Japanese manufacturers – Suzuki, Kawasaki, Yamaha and Honda – have yet to show much interest in the category. That does not stop the racers from entering, however, and most competitors choose either Suzuki or Kawasaki powerplants.

The progress of the category can be charted by the performance of one man: Terry Vance. Vance, with engine builder and business partner Byron Hines, dominated the category from its inception in 1979. Vance won 27 NHRA National event titles during his career – he retired at the end of the 1988 season – and is yet to be caught by his racing rivals. At the end of the 1991 season, the rider coming closest to Vance's career-victory record was former rival David Schultz who, ironically, rides the Vance & Hines Racing Team Kawasaki. He had 15 National event titles in a riding career that spanned the same time as Vance's.

Apart from his numerous victories, Vance recorded the category's first seven-second run, 7.99 seconds – again at the Motorplex – and even ran in the sixes at more than 200 mph (321.86 km/h) on his Suzuki Top Fuel Bike.

When Vance retired, many people though that Schultz, who had been Vance's nearest rival throughout the mid-1980s, would take over as resident Pro Stock Bike king.

But this was not to be.

▼ **Of all the men who have climbed onto a drag racing motorcycle, none has been as successful as Terry Vance. Vance retired from active competition in 1988, but along the way he collected victories at 27 National events.**

PRO STOCK MOTORCYCLE

As the only two-wheel category recognized by the NHRA, Pro Stock Motorcycle is a class in which Japanese performance meets American ingenuity. Built around a rigid frame and cloaked in carbon-fibre body panels, the petrol-burning motorcycles travel from zero to 175 mph (281.63 km/h) in 7.6 seconds.
They accelerate so hard that a top rider like 1990 Winston Champion John Myers is moving at 145 mph (233.35 km/h) within 660 feet (200 m) of the starting line.
NHRA National Elapsed-time Record: 7.615 seconds – John Myers, Texas Motorplex, Ennis, Texas, October 1991.
NHRA National Speed Record: 176.47 mph – John Mafaro, Indianapolis Raceway Park, Indianapolis, Indiana, September 1989.
All National Records must be backed up within 1 per cent.

Pizza restaurateur John Mafaro introduced a rigid-framed Suzuki Katana at the 1989 Supernationals and proceeded to run the category's first 7.8- and 7.7-second times. He was also the first rider to go at more than 170 mph (273.58 km/h) on a Pro Stock Bike and easily won that year's Winston Championship. But even as Mafaro got his name into the record books, the winds of change were already blowing through the class.

Georgia engine builder George Bryce put John Myers on his Suzuki GSXR, and almost overnight they became the category's hottest combination. With Myer's natural riding talent and Bryce's undoubted engine-tuning expertise, the pair set about re-writing the record books, dropping the National Record from 7.74 to 7.73 to 7.69 to a stunning 7.615 by the end of the 1991 season.

Mafaro retained his speed Record of 176.47 mph (283.99 km/h), recorded at the 1989 U.S. Nationals, at the close of the 1991.

▲ The Pro Stock Motorcycles are not contested at every NHRA National event, but when they are they fly. The quickest lap recorded by a two-wheeler is John Myers' 7.615, achieved at the 1991 Chief Nationals.

▶ The fastest man on two wheels is John Mafaro, who recorded a 177-mph (284.85-km/h) lap on his Suzuki Katana at the 1991 Gatornationals.

COMPETING ON ALCOHOL

★ ★ ★

Racers have known for years that one of the more efficient ways to achieve instant performance is to bolt a supercharger on top of the engine. Feed the combination a nitromethane mixture and you have an instant horsepower powerplant.

However, nitromethane is an expensive fuel, costing more than $40 per gallon ($10 per litre). In one five-second blast, a Top Fuel or Funny Car can use up to 15 gallons (56.78 litres). To allow racers who wanted to run such cars without the cost, NHRA introduced Pro Comp, a category of dragsters and Funny Cars that looked almost identical to their nitro-burning cousins but had one small – and important – difference: the fuel they burned. In Pro Comp, the only allowed fuel was alcohol/methanol.

NHRA introduced Pro Comp in 1973, and through a complicated set of weight limits and engine combinations, dragsters and Funny Cars competed in the same class. In 1982, that idea was scrapped, and by 1983 the two types of hot rods were competing in separate divisions. Today, Alcohol Dragster is considered the breeding ground for tomorrow's Top Fuel stars, and Alcohol Funny Car often produces some of tomorrow's future nitro Funny Car racers.

▼ ▼ **The blown-Alcohol Altered was eventually legislated out of competition, much to the dismay of racers and fans alike. The breed's last triumph came at the 1981 Sportsnationals when Frank Manzo drove his AA/A all the way to the Pro Comp eliminator winner's circle.**

▼ **In late 1991 Pat Austin had a career change: he went Top Fuel racing. But much to the dismay of his competitors, he did not leave his multi-event winning Alcohol Funny Car. By late September 1991, all of Austin's 42 career victories had come in the competitive Alcohol Funny Car ranks.**

ALCOHOL DRAGSTER

Featuring cars virtually identical in appearance to their fuel (nitro) counterparts the Top Fuel dragsters, Alcohol Dragster is open to supercharged cars that burn alcohol/methanol and have three-speed transmissions. The category is controlled by a series of weight limits, and the most popular engine size is 420 cubic inches (6.9 litres). Fuel-injected dragsters burning nitromethane can run in this class, although until recently they had been considered uncompetitive. That line of thought changed when 19-year-old Brooks Brown drove his father's Fuel Dragster to a 5.89-second lap at the 1991 Chief Nationals in mid-October.
NHRA National Elapsed-time Record: 5.891 seconds – Brooks Brown, Texas Motorplex, Ennis, Texas, October 1991.
NHRA National speed Record: 234.13 mph – Tom Conway, Houston Raceway Park, Houston, Texas, December 1990.
All National Records must be backed up within 1 per cent.

▶ **The Alcohol Dragsters look like their fuel counterparts, but instead of burning nitromethane they use methanol and have a three-speed transmission.**

CASTROL GTX ALCOHOL 5-SEC CLUB

Open to the first eight drivers in Alcohol Dragster and the first eight in Alcohol Funny Car to record a sub-six-second time, the Castrol GTX Alcohol 5-Second Club indicated how quickly drag-racing performance progressed through the 1980s – at the beginning of the decade, Top Fuel dragsters were struggling to run five-second laps with any consistency.

1	BOB NEWBERRY	5.952	7 May 1989 (Funny Car)
2	PETER GALLEN	5.978	7 May 1989 (Funny Car)
3	STEVE FARIA	5.994	27 May 1989 (dragster)
4	DENNIS ALLEN	5.989	29 July 1989 (dragster)
5	BILL BARNEY	5.945	30 July 1989 (dragster)
6	TOM CONWAY	5.916	12 Aug. 1989 (dragster)
7	PAT AUSTIN	5.985	4 Sept. 1989 (Funny Car)
8	MIKE KOSKY	5.961	17 Sept. 1989 (dragster)
9	JACKIE STIDHAM	5.983	29 Sept. 1989 (Funny Car)
10	BLAINE JOHNSON	5.911	5 Oct. 1989 (dragster)
11	JAY PAYNE	5.961	5 Oct. 1989 (dragster)
12	BRAD ANDERSON	5.968	7 Oct. 1989 (Funny Car)
13	STAN SIPOS	5.977	18 May 1990 (Funny Car)
14	ROGER PRIMM	5.997	28 July 1990 (dragster)
15	FRANK MANZO	5.991	15 Sept. 1990 (Funny Car)
16	DAVE SEBRING	5.977	28 Sept. 1990 (Funny Car)

Despite competing in separate categories, both types of car have remarkably similar performances. By the end of the 1991 season, Blaine Johnson was the Alcohol Dragster performance leader with a 5.872-second time, and Pat Austin was the undisputed Alcohol Funny Car king with a 5.853-second best. Considering that at the beginning of the 1980s most Top Fuel cars could not achieve that kind of performance, the alcohol cars have come a long way.

Although other racers have gone quicker, the undisputed barrier breaker in the alcohol ranks is Bob Newberry, who races an Alcohol Funny Car. He was the first driver into the five-second zone with a 5.952-second time at Old Bridge Township Raceway in Englishtown, N.J., in May 1989; he was the first to run more than 230 mph – 230.59 mph (371.09 km/h) – in March of the same year, and he was the first to go more than 240 mph with a 240.44 mph (386.94 km/h) at the Summernationals in July 1991.

▼**Pat Austin may have the most wins, but Bob Newberry is the Alcohol Funny Car barrier breaker. Newberry was the first alcohol racer** into the five-second zone, first over 230 mph (370.14 km/h), and first over 240 mph (386.23 km/h).

▲ **When it comes to all-out Alcohol Dragster performance, Californian Blaine Johnson is the man to beat in his and brother Alan's Oldsmobile-powered entry.**

ALCOHOL FUNNY CAR

From the outside, there is little, if any, difference between an Alcohol Funny Car and a nitro-burning Funny Car. The big difference is under the fibreglass bodywork. Alcohol Funny Car racers use engines in excess of 520 cubic inches (8.5 litres), their fuel-burning cousins are restricted to a 500-cubic-inch (8.2 litres) maximum. Burning an alcohol/methanol combination and using three-speed transmissions, the cars' current performance marks are in the low 5.9-second range with average speeds around 235 mph (378.19 km/h).

NHRA National Elapsed-time Record: 5.853 seconds — Pat Austin, Houston Raceway Park, Houston, Texas, March 1991.

NHRA National speed Record: 239.04 mph — Pat Austin, Houston Raceway Park, Houston, Texas, March 1991.

All National Records must be backed up within 1 per cent.

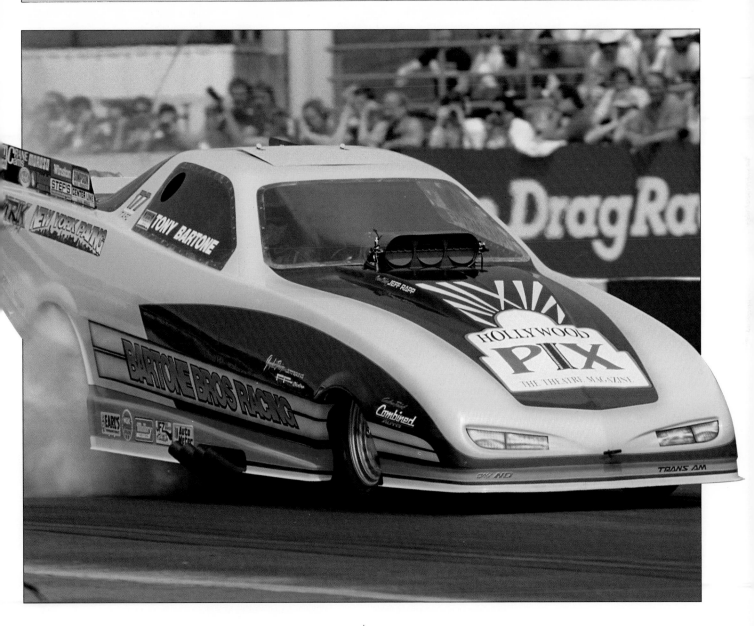

▲ **Strikingly similar to their nitro-burning cousins, Alcohol Funny Cars run much larger capacity engines — anything up to 540 cubic** inches (8.8 litres) — and are among the most competitive of all the classes contested in drag racing.

EIGHT

AROUND THE WORLD –
IN UNDER SIX SECONDS

For a sport uniquely North American – and a motorsport at that – drag racing has become popular in many countries. Nations with active drag-racing programmes include Australia, Britain, Denmark, Finland, France, Germany, Ireland, the Netherlands, New Zealand, Norway, South Africa and Sweden.

The main centres of non-American drag-racing activity are Australia and Northern Europe. Racers in both areas began showing an interest in the sport in the early 1960s, and straight-line activity has been nurtured to varying degrees of stability in each. As the sport moves into the mid-1990s, Australia is the most developed centre of drag racing. The Australian National Drag Racing Association (ANDRA) boasts an event and racer-support programme that rivals that of the NHRA (on which it is loosely based).

COMPETITION ELIMINATOR

Utilizing a handicap starting system in which slower cars are given a head start against faster cars, Competition Eliminator races petrol-burning dragsters, altereds, and supercharged coupes and sedans. All use a variety of engines, ranging from tiny 4- and 6-cylinder engines to powerful V-8s that would not be out of place in a Pro Stock car.

▼ **Drag racing is open to many racers in many classes. One of the most complicated classes is Competition Eliminator, in which Texan David Nickens – the 1991 Winston Champion – still reigns supreme.**

▶ **Competition highlights a variety of petrol-burning dragsters, altereds, supercharged coupes and sedans. The class is equalized through a complicated set of weight limits and performance Index controls.**

AUSTRALIAN RULES
★ ★ ★

Under the watchful eye of former racer and ANDRA National Director Tony Thornton, drivers race in front of crowds of 20,000 or more for prize money and contingency purses. The organisation, formed in 1974, crowns its champions each year, much like NHRA's Winston Champions, and the sport enjoys considerable media coverage.

To better serve its racers, the ANDRA divided the sport into four groups. Group One is for heads-up categories and includes the sport's glamour classes: Top Fuel, Funny Car, Pro Stock, Pro Comp (encompassing Alcohol Dragster, Alcohol Funny Car and Alcohol Altered), Pro Stock Bike and Top Bike.

Group Two is reserved for those who race against Class Records or, more simply, it is handicap racing governed by Indexes similar to those used in NHRA Competition Eliminator. Group Two is made up of the Australian version of Competition Eliminator, Super Stock and Competition Bike. Group Three is also a handicap-only collection, reserved for Modified Eliminator, Super Sedan/Super Street (not to be confused with NHRA Super Street) and Modified Bike. Group Four is for heads-up, fixed Index categories, such as Super Gas (9.90 Index).

SUPER STOCK

Featuring American production cars with limited modifications, Super Stockers are perhaps the true factory hot rods. One of the more popular categories in drag racing, it includes entries ranging from late-model cars that appear almost street legal to vintage big-engined cars from the 1960s and 1970s.

▲ Super Stock features American production cars with limited modifications. In order to equalize competition, cars that run in a slower, less powerful class are given a head start.

READ ALL ABOUT IT
★ ★ ★

At the beginning of the 1980s Australian drag racing was dominated by one man: Top Fuel driver Jim Read. In a career that has spanned four decades, Read has won every major Australian drag-racing title at least once. At the beginning of the decade, he was also the quickest and fastest Australian drag racer with personal bests of 6.19 seconds and 234.36 mph (377.16 km/h) recorded at Castlereagh Dragstrip in New South Wales.

Despite several pretenders to his throne, Read remained the king of Australian drag racing until 1991, when he was unable to match Romeo Capitanio's performance. During the 1980s, several racers challenged Read's dominance of the Top Fuel category, including John Maher, who just missed making the first five-second run south of the equator when he recorded a tantalizingly close 6.000 at Castlereagh in April 1980. Read, however, remained unshaken by Maher's impressive performances and broke into the five-second zone with a 5.998 in his Winfield-backed dragster on 8 November 1980, again at Castlereagh.

One reason for Read's competitiveness during the early to mid-1980s was international competition from some of North America's top drag racers. The highlight of many Australian seasons was the December/January tours of the continent by racers the calibre of Gary Beck, Marvin Graham, Jeb Allen and Lucille Lee. Read and many other racers were able to learn from their American counterparts and transfer that knowledge to the track.

THE GOODYEAR EAGLE 5-SEC CLUB

The Goodyear Eagle 5-Second Club was open to the first 10 racers to record a sub-six-second lap on the Australian continent. By coincidence, the club is split equally between five Top Fuel dragsters and five Funny Cars, demonstrating how both categories grew at the same pace through the 1980s. Two non-Australians are in the club because of their five-second performances on the Australian continent, Garth Hogan from New Zealand and Al Hofmann from the United States.

1	JIM READ	5.998	8 Nov. 1980 (dragster)
2	LARRY ORMSBY	5.903	21 Nov. 1982 (dragster)
3	GRAEME COWIN	5.950	29 June 1986 (Funny Car)
4	AL HOFMANN	5.840	7 Feb. 1987 (Funny Car)
5	JIM WALTON	5.920	21 Jan. 1989 (Funny Car)
6	GARTH HOGAN	5.810	11 Feb. 1989 (dragster)
7	ROMEO CAPITANIO	5.820	16 Dec. 1989 (Funny Car)
8	PETER RUSSO	5.960	24 Feb. 1990 (Funny Car)
9	JOE D'AMATO	5.953	4 March 1990 (dragster)
10	LOUIE RAPISARDA	5.730	31 March 1990 (dragster)

STOCK

Enveloping everything from late-model passenger cars to the popular vehicles of the 1960s and 1970s, Stock is drag racing's purest class. Few modifications are allowed to cars in this class, which is often a racer's first taste of drag-racing competition. Slower machines are given head starts.

◀ Jim Read has won every Australian drag racing title at least once in his long and varied career. In 1982 he travelled to the United States to compete at the Winternationals, and surprised all when he qualified his hastily put together dragster on the pole position.

▲ Stock covers everything from late-model passenger cars to vehicles of the 1950s and 1960s. Few modifications are allowed in this entry-level class.

After beating Graham during the first part of 1981, Read felt confident enough to organize a racing trip to North America to compete at the 1982 NHRA Winternationals. Despite numerous problems, including having to virtually rebuild the race car he had been promised would be ready to roll, Read qualified on the pole at that race with a 5.698-second run. However, his tour ended in the first round when Allen defeated him.

Read returned to racing in Australia, and despite flashes of brilliance from other racers, he has since ruled the roost. He made his way into the record books with laps of 5.945 (April 1982), 5.82 (April 1983), 5.65 (February 1989), 5.52 (April 1989) and 5.47 (January 1990).

The apparent lack of record-breaking by Read during the mid-1980s can be attributed to one factor: lack of interest in Top Fuel, a similar fate that temporarily befell the class in the U.S. at roughly the same time.

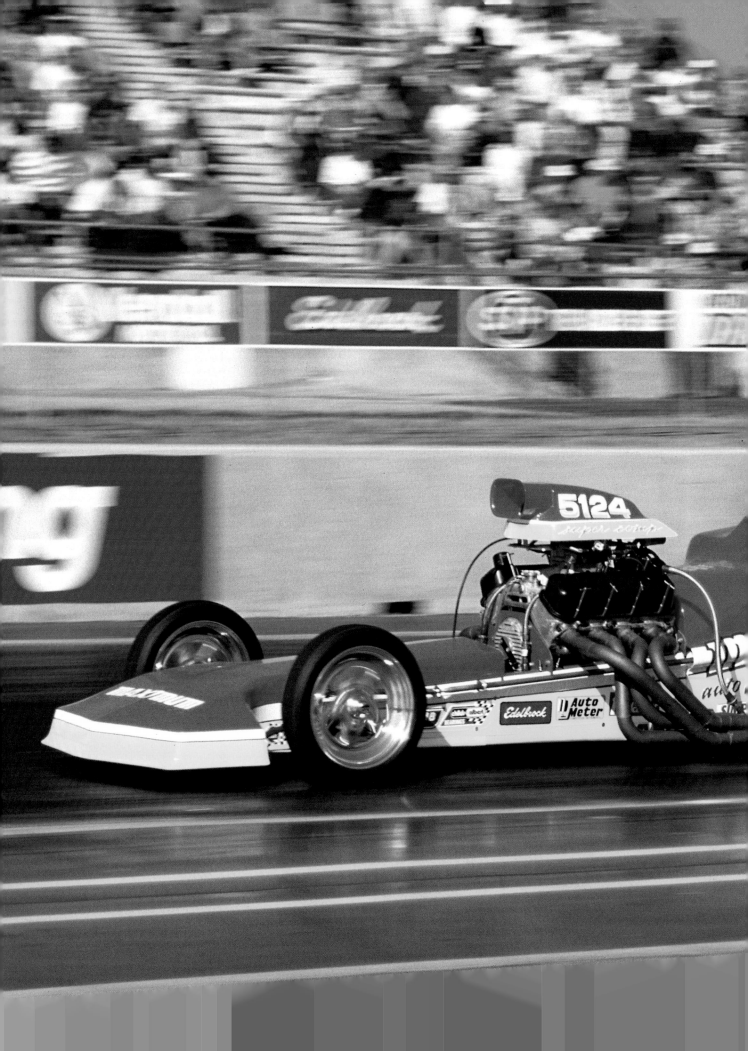

◄ **Super Comp is open to petrol-burning dragsters, altereds and sedans, but with a catch. They cannot go quicker than an 8.90-second Index. Apart from that small restriction, the class is virtually unlimited.**

NOT SO FUNNY
★ ★ ★

During this time, another Australian stamped his name on the scene: Graeme Cowin. Cowin, a former Fuel Altered racer, had been campaigning Funny Cars since the mid-1970s. During the mid-1980s, he became Australia's most popular drag-racing star. Like Read, who regularly beat the visiting American racers in Top Fuel, Cowin overcame the American Funny Car racers. Among the prized scalps he claimed during the 1980s were those of Mike Dunn, Jim Dunn, Tim Grose and Rocky Epperley. Much like Read, Cowin's achievements came at a record-breaking pace.

Entering the decade, Cowin held the all-time best Funny Car marks at 6.56 seconds and 217.38 mph (349.83 km/h), which he recorded in his Camaro-bodied entry at Castlereagh Dragstrip. Cowin lowered that time to a 6.35 in March 1982 at the wheel of Ed Stipanovich's Mustang. Two cars (both Camaros; both destroyed in fires) and two-and-a-half-years later, Cowin dropped the record even further to a 6.32 in his new Pontiac Trans Am-bodied entry.

In January 1985, American racer Grose lowered the record to 6.18 and then 6.11 before Cowin came back with a 6.06. Two months later, Cowin was on the threshold of the fives; he recorded a 6.04 against another American racer, Epperley. Bolstered by his at-home success, Cowin headed east for North America to finish the 1985 season. In doing so, he became the most prominent non-American racer to make an impression on the NHRA Winston tour – before or since.

After warming up at an IHRA race, Cowin qualified for the prestigious NHRA U.S. Nationals in his first attempt, then lost a close race to a supercharger-exploding John Force in the first round. Unlike Read, who had been a novelty in 1982 when he came to the Winternationals, Cowin was considered a threat by American racers. They realized that Cowin was a competitive racer who would upset the status quo given half a chance.

It took another 18 months, but that chance came at the 1987 Winternationals, when Cowin returned to the United States and advanced all the way to the final round before losing to reigning Winston Funny Car Champion Kenny Bernstein when his engine broke a couple of connecting rods. Through the end of the 1991 racing season, Cowin's runner-up finish remains the best performance by a non-North American drag racer in more than 14 years. (Britain's Clive Skilton scored a runner-up finish in the Top Fuel final at the 1977 Springnationals. He lost to Shirley Muldowney, who was on the way to her first of three Winston Top Fuel Championship.)

SUPER COMP
Open to petrol-burning dragsters, American production cars and roadsters, Super Comp is run on an 8.90-second Index with breakouts and heads-up starts. Engine modification is virtually unlimited; the driver's main concern is running the Index. Racers making passes quicker than the prescribed number are eliminated from competition.

◄ For the early part of the 1980s Graeme Cowin was Australia's leading driver. However, when the local competition became too weak, he took his racing operation to the United States to compete with the sport's best.

► Although Don Prudhomme currently campaigns a Top Fuel dragster, he made his reputation in the Funny Car ranks, winning the Winston Funny Car Championship for four consecutive years.

◄ and ► **With sponsorship from Graeme Cowin's Rocket Industries concern, Romeo Capitanio has emerged as Australia's leading drag racer. By mid-1991 Capitanio held performance records in both Top Fuel dragster and Funny Car.**

► **With Graeme Cowin as his sponsor and mentor, Romeo Capitanio has become Australia's leading drag racer as the sport moves into the 1990s.**

Between his stays in the U.S., Cowin continued to race in his home country. In July 1986, he recorded the first five-second time on the continent by a Funny Car, achieving a 5.95 while match racing U.S. driver Gary Densham at Willowbank Raceway in South Queensland.

At the beginning of the new decade, Cowin had retired, and Read was recovering from a bad crash at Willowbank in August 1990. Australian drag racing in general was still affected by a huge loss suffered in 1984 when Castlereagh Dragstrip was closed in the name of urban development, leaving the country's most populous state without a permanent drag-racing facility. However, in late 1989, rumours began to circulate about a new track just minutes from Sydney. Plans to build Eastern Creek Raceway set racers building new cars, and on 25 October 1991 the new track opened its doors.

With the promise of a new track, new racers began to emerge, the most notable of whom was Capitanio. For a while, Capitanio posed no threat to Read, who still dominated the Top Fuel scene during the late 1980s. Aided by Cowin's undoubted tuning expertise, Capitanio became the hottest Australian Funny Car racer since Cowin. Driving a Chevrolet Beretta-bodied entry sponsored by Cowin's Rocket Industries business, Capitanio forced the Funny Car record down 5.62 before turning his attentions to Top Fuel in time for the 1991 Australian Drag Racing Nationals, hosted by Willowbank. Despite never having driven a Top Fuel dragster in his still-short career, Capitanio recorded laps of 5.311 and 5.263 to establish new marks for the class.

◄ Super Gas is reserved for full-bodied cars with mudguards, bonnets, windscreens and functional doors. Again, the class is governed by a performance Index, like Super Comp, only this time the magic number is 9.90 seconds.

BACK FROM THE DEAD

★ ★ ★

If ever a category looked dead and buried in European drag racing during the 1980s, it was Top Fuel. Throughout the mid-1980s, no Top Fuel dragsters existed in Britain, and only a handful sat in workshops in Europe. The class appeared to be on its last legs in other parts of the world, but in Britain it had died.

The reasons for Top Fuel's demise are many, not least of which is the sheer expense of running the thirsty, parts-happy cars. Also, in Europe at least, drag-racing promoters believed that the public wanted to see Funny Cars, and Top Fuel was quietly – but effectively – filtered out of the European system.

That move was typical of the way European drag racing – and the sport in Britain in particular – has stumbled from one trend to another, lacking direction and resources to provide a stable base on which competitors could work. Only in the late 1980s did Scandinavian racers agree to combine their respective rule books, enabling racers from Norway, for example, to travel to racetracks in Sweden or Finland and know that their vehicles were legal for competition.

This situation was a sorry state of affairs because when the sport was first introduced in Britain in 1963 – by way of a tour arranged by NHRA founder Wally Parks that included racers the calibre of Don Garlits – hopes were high that the professionalism of the still fledgling NHRA could be matched.

In the late 1970s, drag racing in Europe was the proverbial beehive of activity. Winston Funny Car Championship-calibre racers such as Don Prudhomme, Raymond Beadle and Gene Snow were regular visitors to Britain to do battle with local drivers. At the 1979 Santa Pod Raceway World Finals, Snow and Beadle recorded the quickest side-by-side Funny Car race in the world with respective times of 6.02 and 6.00. The future promised much; it ultimately delivered little.

British drag-racing stars were few and far between. One of those few lead players was Dennis Priddle, who had burst on the racing scene in the late 1960s and pretty much dominated it after then. Priddle began the 1980s by racing Funny Cars – the only class the promoters wanted – but switched to Top Fuel dragsters in the early 1980s to meet the challenge of the fast-emerging Scandinavians.

Priddle dipped in and out of the five-second zone in his Top Fueler, as did his chief rival, Sweden's Monica Oberg. The two staged infre-

▲ **The Scandinavians dominate the European racing scene. Another female racer, Monica Oberg, has long been a favourite with Swedish fans in her Bosch-baked dragster.**

SUPER GAS

Reserved for full-bodied cars with full mudguards, windscreens and functional doors, Super Gas is the most popular category in NHRA National event competition, accounting for almost 20 per cent of all entries. The class is governed by the same rules as those in Super Comp and Super Street; only the Index, 9.90 seconds, is different.

◀ and ▼ Norwegian Liv Berstad is Europe's leading racer. Driving Rune Fjeld's Mobil 1 Top Fueler she recorded the quickest time ever by a European at 5.13 seconds in September 1990.

▲ One of the newest classes to NHRA National event competition, Super Street caters for production cars that run against a 10.90-second Index.

SUPER STREET

The newest class to be introduced into National event competition, Super Street, like Super Gas, is reserved for full-bodied American production vehicles with full mudguards, bonnets, windscreens and functional doors. A heads-up Pro starting system is used, and runs under the 10.90-second Index are not permitted.

▼ The 1991 season saw the debut of the European Top Fuel Series. It was contested by some of Europe's best drivers across four countries, and Sweden's Tony Bryntesson was one of the drivers pressing for honours.

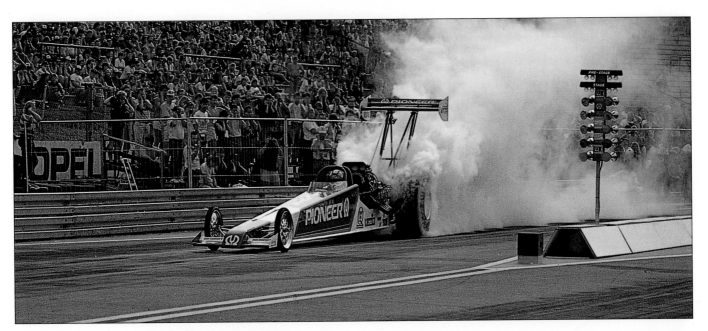

quent battles across Europe until 1987, when Priddle called it quits with a 5.82-second best to his credit. He said he could no longer afford to race. True to his word, Priddle never drove a dragster again.

Although Priddle's departure left a void in British Top Fuel racing circles – he was the only racer in the class at the time – Oberg had already sown the seeds in Scandinavia, where several Nordic racers emerged from the shadows to challenge for Europe's quickest racer title. Among them were Sweden's Pelle Lindelow and Tony Bryntesson,

and, towards the end of the decade, Norwegian racer Liv Berstad.

Berstad, financial director of Scandinavia's largest contemporary clothing company, had cut her teeth in a Pro Stock car but found her home in one of Rune Fjeld's ex-Joe Amato Top Fuel dragsters. The female driver quickly became Europe's quickest racer, getting down into the 5.40-second zone, then the 5.30s, 5.20s and, ultimately, the 5.1s with a magnificent 5.13, recorded at Santa Pod Raceway in Bedford, England, in 1990.

TURNING THE PAGE

★ ★ ★

Priddle's retirement in 1986 left a noticeable gap in British drag racing. Alan Herridge – known during the 1970s as the English "Big Daddy" – was Priddle's natural successor to the throne, but he had died in a jet-car accident at Santa Pod in November 1982. Stepping into Priddle's shoes was one of the sport's young contenders: Gary Page.

Page began his drag-racing career by driving a succession of Competition Eliminator altereds, which he and brothers David and Clive owned. After being dominant in the altered ranks during the mid-1970s,

the brothers took the plunge and went alcohol racing. They drove an Alcohol Altered with great success.

Having proved themselves masters of that category, they decided to go Funny Car racing, ironically with an ex-Dennis Priddle entry. During that period, Gary, the youngest of the brothers, established a solid reputation as favourite with the British fans.

Teaming with former Competition Eliminator racer Bob Jarrett in 1987, Page became one of the first British Funny Car racers in the five-second zone and ultimately recorded the best time by a British Funny Car driver, 5.85 seconds, in 1990.

◄ **Britain's leading drivers are in the Funny Car ranks, with Gary Page being the class's top exponent. Driving an ex-Tom Hoover entry, Page recorded numerous high-5-second runs at tracks around Europe.**

One success story in European drag racing is the Nordic Pro Stock Racers Association. Despite being introduced into Scandinavia only in the late 1980s, Pro Stock has become the most popular Professional category in European drag racing, boasting more than 30 entries across northern Europe.

Competition within the category is close; a 16-car field is usually separated by less than half a second. The leading racer is Norwegian Per-Kristian Skinne, whose 1987 Pontiac Trans Am entry went undefeated for more than two years in Europe before dropping a race to American Morris Johnson Jnr. at the Motopark, near Helsinki, Finland.

Skinne has also raced in North America on numerous occasions and qualified for the 1990 NHRA Gatornationals in Florida. He remains the only non-North American racer to qualify for an NHRA Pro Stock show in National event history.

▲ One of the success stories in European drag racing has been the formation of the Nordic Pro Stock Racers. Consisting of drivers from countries such as Sweden, Norway and Finland, the series is one of the most professional contested anywhere in the world.

GOOD TIMES
★ ★ ★

The one factor that affects all drag racers outside the North American continent is that the sport is uniquely American. It is loud, brash and ultimately very expensive. Import duties and shipping costs can make the sport prohibitively expensive for all but the most dedicated racer. It is, therefore, a tribute to the respective wills of non-American drag racers that the sport not only exists outside America, but also flourishes.

INDEX

PICTURE CREDITS

Apart from the following exceptions, all photographs used in this book (including those on the jacket) are reproduced courtesy of Leslie Lovett. Jon van Daal: pp 118, 119; Andy Willshire: pp121, 122, 123 (bottom).